How to Star[t a] Business as a Private Tutor

Set up a tutoring business from home

Learn the secrets of success from years of experience
in tuition from primary through to GCSEs
Free ready to use printable forms and sample adverts

Graham Woodward

Skills Training Course
www.UoLearn.com

How to Start a Business as a Private Tutor

Set up a tutoring business from home

Learn the secrets of success from years of experience in tuition from primary through to GCSEs
Free, ready to use, printable forms and sample adverts

(Skills training course)

Published by: Universe of Learning Ltd, reg number 6485477, Lancashire, UK
www.UoLearn.com, support@UoLearn.com

First Published 2010

ISBN 978-1-84937-029-5

Cover picture by Yuri Arcurs, www.fotolia.com

Photographs by various artists, © www.fotolia.com

Dedication

To Kathleen

I would like to dedicate this book to my lovely wife who has brought me so much happiness. She has shown me unconditional patience, understanding and encouragement, and has had to 'live' with me while I compiled this book. During my many moods and disappearances to my office, she has kept me supplied with endless cups of tea.

Thank you, my love

Acknowledgments

I would like to thank Tina who had the unenviable task of trying to read and understand my handwriting. Despite her physical difficulties she did a first class job of typing out my original script; except for her 'phobia' of the letter 'S' which her surgeon is concerned about and may hopefully correct.

There are many people, over the years, who have given me the inspiration to succeed – and I thank them all; none more so than my mother and father, who have not only been excellent parents, but also my employers. They have given me a first class apprenticeship not only in engineering, but in life skills too.

Not many people can say they have met their heroes. I am lucky in that respect - I have met and talked with three out of four of mine. Sir Matt Busby, Roy Orbison and Sir John Harvey-Jones have all inspired me in different ways. Unfortunately Mozart died before I was born.

A special thanks to Mr E. C. Rigg MBE. AFC. (my Uncle Ted) who I have respected and held in high esteem since early childhood. His help, advice and criticism were greatly appreciated in proof reading the original draft.

I would like to thank Dave and Mike for dragging me into the 21st century and for their help in production of the original manual.

Finally, I am grateful to Margaret Greenhall for all her help in making such a professional job of the book you are now going to enjoy.

About the Author
Graham Woodward

Graham was born in 1947, peculiarly called the 'bulge' year – presumably named because everyone involved in the war celebrated the victory on coming home in the traditional way of the times. Graham was brought up and educated in a time when education meant something, in the 'good' old days of polio, impetigo, televisions with nine inch screens, and enough malt and cod liver oil stuck to your balaclava to last until playtime. Fortunately his liberty bodice and knitted tank top prevented him from falling victim to diphtheria and TB. Enough of the humour; as anyone under the age of 50 reading this will wonder what on earth is being discussed.

After leaving school he joined his father's engineering company as an apprentice, quickly progressing to draughtsman and eventually to works manager. He was one of the youngest people ever to be given full membership of the BIM (British Institute of Management) at 22 years of age and subsequently sat on the London Chamber of Commerce Examining Board representing the BIM executive committee.

He joined a televised sports publicity company as their northern area manager and completely turned the branch around; designing and implementing many new concepts. In 1985 he became managing director of his own company, servicing many lucrative contracts at major nationwide sports venues and events.

Following a long and varied career in management from the age of 20, Graham began to get involved in career advice, training and recruitment. He managed an executive recruitment company specialising in business and technical appointments. This led to him lecturing in further education colleges, teaching BTEC and City and Guilds in engineering, mathematics and science. He has written and marked final exam papers for both these institutions.

Graham has frequently featured in national magazine articles and the education columns of newspapers.

Also an accomplished graphologist, Graham has given lectures and practical demonstrations to professional business groups on this subject. In addition to analysing the handwriting of a number of celebrities, he is seconded to several companies who use his skills to have the CV's of prospective candidates analysed.

He has worked in many secondary schools, supporting statemented and special needs children and also liaising with their parents. In 1992 he began to tutor children individually in their own homes. This quickly became a lucrative occupation leading to the formation of his own company. Graham is in great demand, not only to tutor children privately, but also to train people from all walks of life who wish to embark on a new and rewarding career.

Graham can be contacted at www.gpwtutoring.co.uk or via graham@uolearn.com

*Training course

We hope that you enjoy this book and that it helps you to become a tutor. If you want more help you might like to consider the face to face course that Graham offers. It is an intensive one-to-one training package over two days where everything is supplied for you to start a very lucrative business of your own.

During the training session Graham spends two days with you including one night where you accompany him visiting several of his tutees, in their own homes and meet their parents. You can see first hand how it is done, take notes, pick up tips and discuss things with Graham as you go along.

As part of the course you'll be given a briefcase full of everything you'd be likely to need as a home tutor and an assortment of useful books and work sheets.

One of the most special things about taking part in the two day course is that you have unlimited support from Graham to help you set up your business.

Please do contact Graham via his website www.gpwtutoring.co.uk for further details.

*Please note these are services provided by the author.
The publishers, Universe of Learning Limited, have no liability, responsibility or involvement regarding these events and resources.

Great comments

"I'm busy planning how to advertise and hope I'll be able to get going very soon. Thank you for all your helpful advice and for the material you provided me with. I still feel quite nervous about starting but also quite excited about the possibilities tutoring offers."

"Since seeing Graham my twins have really come on, without his help they would have struggled."

"My daughter has improved in maths almost immediately thanks to Graham's unique way of making it sound so simple."

"Your help has turned my life around. I'm now doing something worthwhile."

"You provided me with some great tips on getting started and I purchased a copy of your book.

I'm pleased to say that the business is going well. I have six pupils at present and all are making good progress. The parents are also very happy with the services I'm providing. I am combining this work with supply teaching during the day and working in the local library two days a week to ensure a regular income.

I would like to thank you again. Starting tuition is the best thing I could have done after recovering from my illness and your advice and book have been invaluable."

Contents

About the Author: Graham Woodward	5
Great comments	8
Preface	10
Introduction	11
A question of qualifications	13
School and their Systems Today	19
Acquiring Your Clientbase	24
Websites for Tutors	33
Fees and Potential Income	35
Handling the Initial Response	40
Planning a Timetable	44
First Visit and Assessment	47
Preparation	55
Professionalism	59
How to get an Immediate Improvement	64
Homework - 'to give or not to give?'	70
Statemented and Special Needs Children	73
Home Educating and the Law	79
Media Awareness	86
Exams, Tests and Grammar or Private School Selection	89
Numeracy	95
Literacy	107
Ideas and Tips	116
What could go wrong?	120
Last bits of advice	126
Equipment list	130
Further reading	132
Useful forms	134
Index	141
Further courses and packs	143
About the publisher	146

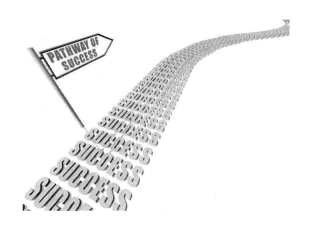

Preface

Thank you for purchasing this book. Here, at last, is the inside story of what to expect, what to do and how to do it. More importantly, this book will tell you what not to do.

It is intended as an informative book packed with sensible, practical advice, written by someone who first hand has made a successful career from tutoring hundreds of children; someone who has a real understanding of underachieving school children and their dissatisfied parents.

Sometimes controversial and outspoken – the author is not afraid to put his views forward, often with a sense of humour.

Are you perhaps over fifty years old and feel you're on the scrap heap? Do you sit at home wasting time applying for jobs you will never get; or are you in a thankless, boring, underpaid job, regardless of age? Are you taking a career break to look after a family and would like a challenge?

The author feels there is a frustrated tutor in many of us. This book will help you put that potential to good use. Within its pages is your chance to discover how valuable you can be to society. It is essential our children are educated to a high standard – this book will enable you to work in tandem with the education system to provide that standard.

Introduction

Private home tuition is a growing, booming business and there has never been a better time to get involved. Education and schools are frequently in the news and media and, it has to be said, many parents are unhappy with their children's lack of progress at school. Many children need extra help urgently and parents are eager to pay for this service. If you think everything is fine in schools today take a few minutes to read the press cuttings in the margins of this book.

Home tuition is not the luxury it once was; it has now become the norm for families from all backgrounds. Some parents are reluctant to admit to using tutors, and some schools see it as interfering, whilst turning a blind eye to something that boosts their results. Nevertheless many children of all ages are being privately tutored on a one-to-one basis in their own homes.

Home tutoring is not the same as school teaching, nor do you have to be a qualified teacher to practise it. One-to-one tutoring is by far more effective than class teaching in a school environment. A tutor can tailor make the work to suit each individual child, resolving any problems as they occur. As you build a close relationship with a child, something that cannot be fostered in a classroom, their confidence will significantly improve.

"Nearly 300 000 children a year leave primary school unable to write properly, inspectors said yesterday.

Fifty-two per cent of 11 year-old boys and 45 per cent of all primary pupils are failing national tests for spelling, punctuation and grammar."

This enables a tutor to discover and bring out any hidden talents and potential the child may have. To help a child improve you must remember your interest and loyalty lie with the child first and then to the parents. They do not lie with the teachers, school or education system.

I will explain how to get started in this lucrative business. Every facet will be discussed in detail based on my experiences in tutoring children and training adults from all walks of life over many years. I will make you aware of any pitfalls or problems you are likely to encounter such as the school system and how parents struggle to cope with it, what children are really like in and out of school and how to handle both bright children and those who have learning difficulties.

If you are in any doubt after reading this book as to whether becoming a tutor is for you, remember the current generation has a duty to ensure that today's children are properly educated. Schools are not, in my opinion, generally doing a good job. Of the many business opportunities you may have previously considered or tried, this will be the most rewarding and worthwhile. It will add to your self esteem and make you feel proud to be a part of our children's future.

Yes, you can do it. Read on and discover all you need to know, that rewarding new career lies ahead.

A question of qualifications

The most frequently asked question from people considering a career as a tutor is

'Do I have to be a qualified teacher?'

NO! You do not have to be qualified.

The Oxford Dictionary definition of a teacher is as follows:

> *"A person who explains, shows and helps to impart knowledge by way of instruction and example."'*

Do you honestly think you need to go to university and wear a gown and a mortar board and obtain a B.Ed. in order to do this?

What do you think every parent does every day with his or her children? As an example, a parent is a very 'qualified' teacher who exercises that 'qualified' role every day.

If you are particularly good at anything – mathematics, gardening, decorating, etc., if you can communicate well, are reasonably intelligent and care about children; who has the audacity to suggest you have to be 'qualified' to impart your knowledge to another person?

A reasonably well-educated adult is perfectly able to pass information to a child, probably better than a teacher is. Parents today are not impressed with schools as they feel they are simply not delivering. Good teachers are swallowed into the system; they have to follow the national curriculum. Teachers inevitably lose their enthusiasm due to the lack of discipline and classroom behaviour of today's children. I actually tutor children whose parents are teachers and they discuss education and their child's progress on the same level. In fact they listen to my ideas and ask my advice. Most are envious of my flexibility in a one-to-one situation as opposed to having to control a rowdy class of thirty children in which only half of them are interested in doing any work.

I know – I have worked in schools, sat in staff rooms and talked to teachers at length. Most of the younger ones have reservations about their teacher training courses and would rather (if they were allowed) exercise more common sense and spend more time with the children who were enthusiastic to learn; rather than constantly trying to control the disruptive ones.

I once asked a teacher years ago, when I was considering starting as a private home tutor, what she thought of me not being a qualified teacher. She said, "**Just go for it!** I don't have to take my car to a qualified mechanic if it breaks down – I can get a friend or a neighbour to look at it if I wish." A good analogy, I thought.

In over ten years of being a private home tutor I have been asked if I was a qualified teacher only three or four times. I always reply politely, "No, I am not, but if you are happy with teachers who are qualified and the school, why are you ringing me?" I offer them references and testimonials from satisfied parents and they are perfectly happy.

Always remember, too, that the last thing a child wants to see knocking at their door at night is a teacher. Of course, parents may want to know something about your background. You may have what you think is an unimportant 'qualification' or experiences that you don't think are relevant – but they are, and you must inform the parents of prospective students. I once trained a forty-nine year old nurse to be a tutor. At first she was apprehensive and felt she wasn't qualified and this worried her more than her ability in basic mathematics (which I put right for her over a day's session). During our meeting and discussion she realised that during her early nursing training she had worked on a ward for long stay children who had needed some form of education during their stay in hospital. She had helped with and enjoyed teaching basic mathematics and English to children aged three to eleven for a period of nine months in a converted day room of the hospital ward. I asked what she thought this was if not valuable experience in communicating with and helping children. I suspect she did a better job than most primary teachers could have done. Here are some further examples of experience you may have had but have not thought relevant:

- ✓ N.N.E.B Qualification.
- ✓ S.S.A (Special Support Assistant) in schools.
- ✓ Unqualified (that word again) assistant in primary schools.
- ✓ Helping friends' children with their homework.
- ✓ Training apprentices in industry.
- ✓ Teaching your own children or grandchildren

Participating on one of our courses obviously will enable you to take up private tuition. Reading this book will give you a good insight into becoming a tutor. Freud (Sigmund, not Clement) once said, "To do is to be." How right he was. If you are doing something and being successful then you become that success, whether you are a mechanic, decorator, estate agent or a private home tutor. Is every teacher a capable and successful one? Yet every teacher is qualified. Would you say, because of those qualifications, they are better than you at teaching and communicating with children? I don't think so. Why are so many schools underachieving? Of course there is good and bad by definition in any establishment or activity, but do you really think you have to go to a university or college to be shown how to teach a child? No, you do not. Do you think you are not going to be as good as a 'qualified' teacher? Think again. As you may have gathered by now I have a big problem with the word 'qualified' – I prefer to say capable or experienced.

You will, of course, need to know what you are talking about from an academic point of view. Most of the children I have

"Noisy classrooms are making teachers unwell as they fight to be heard above the din, scientists claim. Staff forced to raise their voices take more time off due to throat strain and stress."

on my books are lacking basic skills in mathematics and English, subjects you can quickly brush up on if you need to. In subsequent sections, I shall show you examples of various expected levels of attainment and recommended books in mathematics and English for children of different ages.

How you communicate with or tutor children is down to your own personality and patience. If you are a parent you already know how to do this, most of it is common sense anyway. All you need is confidence and know how to put your knowledge across to a child in a professional manner.

Many adults I train say they always wanted to be a teacher – I tell them they already are. Everyone who passes on knowledge to someone else, giving them the skill to do something they previously didn't know how to is, by definition, a teacher. If you re-educate someone so that something they previously had knowledge of, but didn't understand, suddenly becomes accessible to them then you are a tutor. Rather than passing on new knowledge to a child in their own home your remit is to help them with work they have already been taught in school but perhaps failed to fully understand at the time. This is the ethos of home tuition. However, in actual fact you are, in many cases, teaching them something for the first time.

This is because, believe it or not, there is not enough time in schools today (especially primary schools) to teach children all of the national curriculum, let alone to back track or to repeat difficult lessons and concepts until they are fully understood. This is why more and more parents are turning to tutors for help, as a necessity rather than the luxury it was once regarded as. It is a means of ensuring their children 'keep-up' at school or reach the required standards. Are you convinced yet that you don't have to be 'qualified' or a school teacher to offer private home tuition? I hope so, but if I haven't convinced you I suggest you re-read this section until you feel confident.

Exercise:

List 3 qualities that you think you have that will make you a good tutor.

....

....

....

....

....

....

List three skills that you think you need to improve on to start working as a tutor.

....

....

....

....

....

....

Criminal Records Bureau Checks (CRB)/ Independent Safeguarding Authority (ISA) checks

At the time of writing it isn't legally necessary for an individual directly employed by the parents in the UK to get a CRB check. Self employed people can't get a check done directly but there are umbrella organisations which can organise one for you. Some parents may ask about it and you might like to consider getting one done as it may help reassure parents that you have a professional approach to work. However, if you are asked to work with foster children you will need to have one done. The cost is fairly low but it can take up to 8 weeks for the forms to process through the system. The law as of 26th July 2010 will allow self-employed people to register with the ISA. Please visit www.crb.gov.uk or ring 0870 9090811 for the most up-to-date information.

"Can I register with the ISA if I am self employed?

Yes, from 26 July 2010, if you are self employed, work with either children or vulnerable adults and meet the requirements for regulated activity, you can and may choose to register with the ISA. It is not a mandatory requirement to do so, but you may be asked by potential employers to confirm that you are registered to work with children or vulnerable adults.

For example, you may be a tutor carrying out private tuition at family homes; the persons responsible for a child or vulnerable adult to whom you are providing lessons are entitled to ask whether you are registered with the ISA before employing you and not being registered may affect their decision to do so."

Source: http://www.crb.homeoffice.gov.uk/faqs/top_10. aspx#keychanges, Dec 2009

School and their Systems Today

I may have, so far, given the impression that I have no time for teachers or, in fact, that I dislike them. This is not the case; some of my friends are teachers. In fact, I tend to feel sorry for them because of what they have to endure. There is very little discipline evident in schools today, not usually because the teachers fail to attempt to instil it but because the children adamantly reject it. There is no ultimate deterrent in the classroom and so most children who have a flagrant disregard for any sort of authority show no respect whatsoever for the teacher. This results in frequent classroom disruptions and confrontations subjecting the teachers to constant stress when obviously teaching is not taking place; reducing a fifty-minute lesson to thirty minutes of actual teaching at most. I have seen this happening first hand in many classrooms in every school I have worked in.

It sounds Victorian but I strongly believe you cannot educate a child until they are disciplined or made to respect authority i.e. teachers in particular. Without going off at a moral tangent – this is the underlying cause of why society and, in particular, behaviour, has changed to the detriment of us all. Not only teachers suffer – police and many people in authority also find coping with today's children a major problem. Look at the press cuttings elsewhere in this section if you think I am exaggerating. Most, if not all, teachers are trying to do their job under stress but the situation is worse in infant and junior schools where the national curriculum may not have time to be completed before a child reaches year 6 (their final year – at 11 years old).

I believe we should be ensuring our 5 to 11 year olds know the basics of mathematics and English, tables in particular, at the expense of cutting back on ancient Egyptians, volcanoes, butterflies and even French, history, geography and science were always left in the main to be taught in secondary school, anyway.

This obviously causes problems in secondary schools when inheriting struggling children passed on from junior schools. Time is wasted in trying to bring children up to standard in years 7 and 8 (especially in mathematics and English) before academic learning can progress satisfactorily.

Children are sometimes unfortunately streamed or segregated into sets depending on their behaviour rather than their ability. This causes many problems because often clever children can be found in the bottom sets, simply because they would rather misbehave and be seen to be disruptive by their peers.

Case study - disruptive behaviour

I once supported a boy aged 13 who was in the bottom set of a mathematics group. He was particularly disruptive on this day and, despite my efforts to try and control him with reason and mathematical help, the teacher eventually suggested I take him out of the classroom (a regular occurrence) to avoid further disruption. Once I had isolated him in a room I insisted we study mathematics for the remainder of the morning. Not only did his attitude change, he produced (without too much help from me) at least 10 sides of A4 of mathematics problems and calculations. I was amazed by his speed and ability to perform calculations without the aid of a calculator. The headmaster called in to see how he was behaving and, like me, was astounded at his achievement. I suggested that he should be moved up a set in mathematics, as he had proved himself more than able to cope. In fact, he was moved up two sets. He was very proud at first and, of course, his parents were delighted and impressed. Unfortunately, after two months, peer pressure was too strong. He was in danger of losing his mates in the bottom set by being seen to be clever. He started to become disruptive and misbehave once again and was moved back down to the bottom set. I wonder, if he had had private tuition at home in mathematics whether his interest in mathematics would have been kept on track? Ironically, whilst in the higher set, he had also improved in other subjects.

Statemented and special needs children (to be discussed later in detail) are not given enough help in school today due to the lack of funding from local authorities. This applies equally in primary and secondary education. In fact, there are some children who should be getting help yet are not even statemented, due in some cases, to parents not being insistent enough. Some children are sometimes given I.E.P.'s (Individual Education Plans)

"The National Curriculum is divided into key stages, each with work to suit the needs of your growing child."

when it is not necessary because schools receive extra funding for this. The whole system is in disarray – and who suffers most because of this – the children and their disgruntled parents.

Teachers are always under pressure to get the best exam results possible, not just for the pupil's sake but to warrant next year's funding and attract parents to send their children to the school when the new intake is imminent.

In Lancashire we still have the 11+ system or entrance exams for Grammar Schools (either fee paying or free) that many people think is wrong, but I think it is necessary to recognise our bright children as early as possible and send them to Grammar school before the Great in Great Britain disappears completely.

In our present schools the identification of different year groups and key stages can be daunting to parents, let alone to prospective private tutors. Anyone over 40 years old would find this statement completely alien i.e. 'My child is in year 7 and starting key stage 3 work and is already up to level 5!' I hope the following tables will help you to understand the system. It is in year 7, at the age of 11 to 12, that a child starts secondary school.

The present school system is not perfect (no system ever is). Unfortunately, as long as schools and their teachers, local education authorities and government are at loggerheads with each other the children ultimately suffer. This singles out home tuition as the driving force in maintaining education standards.

The years in schools are now numbered sequentially all the way from infants to college entry. However, the first year is not included and is called reception. Children in the UK usually go to school in the year they turn 5 (school years run 1st September to 31st August) so they start school when they are 4 years old which is too young for many to do very much formal learning so this year is usually seen as settling in time. Children starting secondary school now have to stay on until they are 17 years old.

Age at end of year	Current name of year group	Year group in old system	Key stage	Average attainment level at end of stage	Exams
5	reception	infant 1	1		
6	year 1	infant 2	1		
7	year 2	infant 3	1	2	SATs
8	year 3	junior 1	2		
9	year 4	junior 2	2		
10	year 5	junior 3	2		
11	year 6	junior 4	2	4	SATs
12	year 7	year 1	3		
13	year 8	year 2	3		
14	year 9	year 3	3	5 to 6	
15	year 10	year 4	4		GCSE
16	year 11	year 5	4	6 to 7	GCSE
17	year 12	lower 6th	5		AS level
18	year 13	upper 6th	5		A level, Diploma

Table showing UK education levels

The children are divided into key stage groups with a curriculum for each stage. At the end of each of the stages children may take SAT's (statutory assessment tests) and often parents look for a tutor as their child comes up to one of these test dates. For more and current information on the UK system please visit www.direct.gov.uk/en/parents

Acquiring Your Clientbase

People ask 'where do I start?' Quite a few adults I have trained have been thinking of embarking on a career as a tutor for a while before they approach me, perhaps helping neighbours' or friends' children with their homework for free; then realising the potential. That's how I began. If this is the case they are already tutoring without realising it. I'm not suggesting you should suddenly charge a friend £20 per hour when you are tutoring their child already for free, but news spreads quickly and your friend's child will tell their friends – so will the parents.

If you are starting from scratch advertisements in your local paper are best, as large as you can afford. A small box is much more advantageous than any number of lines. Study the sample advertisements I have placed over the years. Feel free to reproduce these or at least to use some of the wording and phraseology. I have experimented with many advertisements and the ones that have brought me most success are here for you to use.

Begin by looking in your local newspapers to see if there is anyone else advertising. If several people are advertising this service, don't worry, most of them will say, 'Help your child with mathematics or English – ring ******.' These take up two lines at most and are not only boring and uninformative but sometimes make the mistake of telling someone they are a 'qualified' (there's that word again) teacher. In my view this is a turn off. Remember my earlier observations regarding qualification.

I also think it gives the wrong impression, if someone appears tight fisted enough to have placed the smallest possible advertisement costing them less than the price of one tutorial (depending obviously on the newspaper). Study my advertising – which person would you phone if you were a parent desperate for help for your child? Another advantage of using a boxed advertisement is these tend to be placed towards the top of the columns, underneath the heading of education/tuition. Therefore all the lineage adverts will be below yours and read last. These, however small, are valuable tips based on my experience over the years. You don't need to spend money experimenting with wording or ad size – I've already done all this for you.

You must change the wording of your advertisements to suit the times for particular tests and examinations that are coming up. One advertisement that regularly appears in our local newspaper always makes me smile – it advertises help for children with their SATs tests in June, July and throughout the summer. The SATs tests are always held in the second week of May, nationally at every school: this again shows unprofessionalism. I advertise in February and March with a direct headline saying 'Is your child ready for the National Tests in May?'

IS YOUR CHILD READY FOR THE NATIONAL TESTS IN MAY?

I guarantee I can get through to your child because I go back to basics
with intensive one-to-one tuition.
I use the old fashioned methods that
schools will not or cannot do anymore!

11+ GRAMMAR SCHOOL TESTS IN NOVEMBER & GCSE EXAMS IN JUNE

7 years old to 17 years old, also adults.
I also have extensive experience in statemented, special needs & children
with behavioural problems.

GET YOUR CHILD UP TO STANDARD NOW!
**REFERENCE & TESTIMONIALS WILLINGLY GIVEN.
I HAVE MANY SUCCESS STORIES**

FOR AN IMMEDIATE IMPROVEMENT RING GRAHAM ON   TO BOOK A NO OBLIGATION ASSESSMENT

Another form of building your client base is to have an A5 leaflet printed. This is something you could quite easily do yourself on coloured paper, or you can get very cheap printing done by companies such as www.vistaprint.co.uk or get them done at your local print shop. You can put these up in sport centres, libraries, doctors' and dentists' waiting rooms; anywhere children and their parents frequent, make sure you ask for permission. Obviously, corner shops, off licences, supermarkets and post offices. I emphasise post offices because of the many different bills you can now pay in them which attract more people than traditional post offices did in the past. Pensioners go there to draw their pensions and mums go to get their benefits. You may not think of aiming your publicity at pensioners but believe me it is vital. Many of the houses I visit are owned by the grandparents of children I tutor. Sometimes I rarely see the parents as they are too busy with work commitments. Grandparents recognise the need for private tuition far more than most parents do. They often collect the child from school, take them back to their home, give them their evening meal and pay for the lesson.

**MATURE STUDENTS & SINGLE PARENTS
ARE YOU WORRIED ABOUT YOUR MATHS?**

Effective Private Intensive Tuition in your own home,
at your convenience.
No need for expensive course fees, bus fares to
college or baby sitters!
One hour per week + homework
maybe all you need.

**FOR AN IMMEDIATE IMPROVEMENT RING
GRAHAM ON   TO BOOK A
NO OBLIGATION ASSESSMENT**

Case study - mail drops

One last word on leaflets – do not put them through doors. When I started out I had 15,000 leaflets printed and, in my naiveté, decided to target a large housing estate nearby that I knew had lots of children living in it. I set off one rainy Sunday morning quite excited at the calls I would get on my return home. The exercise took me over four hours. I even became selective, leaving the homes that obviously didn't have children, with no toys evident; no stickers on the bedroom windows, etc. With hindsight it may have been better to target these as they may have been the homes of grandparents. I was exhausted but very optimistic when I arrived home, despite being very wet. I did not receive one call as a result of my leaflet drop. I repeat, not one. I learned a salutary lesson, which I am gladly passing on to you. I think that by posting a leaflet through a letter box you dilute the perceived quality of your product, which should be above the usual forms of advertising which everyone seems to get i.e. double glazing, pizza take-aways, garden tidying, etc. These are binned! You are selling a professional service and should treat it as such.

FAILED YOUR GCSEs?
POOR GRADES & NEED TO RESIT?

IN BOTTOM SET & HAVE
MOCK GCSEs AT XMAS?

DON'T PANIC!
I CAN HELP WITH INTENSIVE
ONE-TO-ONE TUITION & EXAM
TECHNIQUE.

ALSO FOR STAGE 2: 7-11 YEAR OLDS

For an initial assessment in your
own home call now, testimonials and
references available

FOR AN IMMEDIATE
IMPROVEMENT
RING   DAY OR EVENING

FED UP or WORRIED ABOUT YOUR CHILD'S EDUCATION ?

I GET RESULTS WITH CHILDREN !
TABLES, SPELLINGS, TESTS etc.

JUNIOR KEY STAGE 2: 7-11 YEAR OLDS
UP TO 11+ GRAMMAR SCHOOL EXAM'
GCSEs & MOCKS
ALSO ADULT RECRUITMENT TESTS

For an initial assessment in your own home call now, testimonials and references available

*FOR AN IMMEDIATE IMPROVEMENT RING GRAHAM **** *******

WORRIED ABOUT
GSCEs
NEXT MONTH?

DON'T PANIC
IT'S NOT TOO LATE!

I can help with exam technique and intensive tuition for an immediate improvement.

****

DAYTIME OR EVENING to suit

Phone   Anytime

Probably the best and most effective way of acquiring clients is by word of mouth. Everyone has friends with children or grandchildren. Make sure they all know what you are doing, and give them some leaflets to pass on to their friends. Mums chat at school gates with other mums – it is quite amazing how word spreads. Always have some leaflets (or if you prefer, a simple card) in your car or about your person to pass on to anyone who is remotely interested. If you know someone who runs the cubs, brownies, swimming or judo clubs, make sure they know of your service and have plenty of your leaflets. Knowing someone who is a school governor is also useful for contacting parents whose children need help. Schoolteachers, too, if you know them well enough, are a good source of potential clients.

Be aware, by following the local press, of schools near you that have just had an undesirable or critical OFSTED report or particularly poor exam results. You then need to target parents in that area by placing your leaflet in shops or venues near that school. Do not feel guilty about taking advantage of other people's (i.e. the school's) misfortune. You are satisfying a need for individual parents who are worried about their child's lack of progress at school. Again, study my advertisements; I have spent thousands of pounds advertising over the years. I know which advertisements work well and which do not. I word my ads with the words parents want to read – they are not aimed at teachers or schools. Study the following ads carefully.

Checklist for adverts:

- ❑ What problem are you solving?
- ❑ What type of people is the ad aimed at?
- ❑ Does it say what you offer?
- ❑ Is the message timed correctly - you need to think about 2 to 3 months lead time to important times such as exams.
- ❑ Are your contact details on it telephone, email etc.?
- ❑ Are the contact details correct - check the phone number / email very carefully?
- ❑ Is it all spelled correctly?

Exercise: Design your own ad.

If you don't know the answers for definite yet, just pretend you're aiming at a particular group of people.

What problem are you solving for the client?

....

....

What age will you work with?

....

....

What subjects?

....

....

My advert:

Websites for Tutors

Website building

Most of your business will come from local advertising and word of mouth, so a website is not vital for a tutor. However, it can look very professional to both have a website to refer potential clients to and to use as your email address.

Website design used to be an area for professionals but now it is easy to do. The first thing you need to do is find a web address (url) that is available. If you are UK based try www.123-reg.co.uk or www.hostmonster.com and www.godaddy.com for non-UK sites. On these sites you can put in a potential web address and check whether someone else has bought it already. In terms of endings go for the one that matches your location (e.g. .co.uk for UK, .com for US, .de for Germany etc.). If you buy an address that has not existed before it should be very cheap (about £7 for 2 years on a .co.uk and £8 a year for a .com). Once you've bought your address you then need to buy space to keep your files - this is called hosting (and should be around £30 to £50 for a year). Make sure whichever company you buy the website from also has a website building capability - you don't want to have to spend money paying someone else to do this for you.

It is usually about 24 hours after you've bought your address before you can start putting information into it. So now is the time to be nosy. Just search for other tutors' websites and look at what sort of information they have on them. Look at the layouts and how you navigate through them. Think about the image you want to present to the world - your website should reflect your personality. Write down a sketch of the design and how people will navigate around the site.

Having decided what your site will look like and the content, now you can use the drag and drop website building software that the bigger hosting companies provide. If you want professional looking pictures go to www.fotolia.com or www.shutterstock.com and you can buy pictures with rights to put them in both paper based and web based materials for very low prices.

Once you have a website url you can then use an email address that uses the website address as the ending (like support@uolearn.com) rather than a generic hotmail account. You need to find web forwarding on the hosting provider's site and put in your choice of email address and your normal address. So you won't have to check lots of other email boxes.

Web traffic

Visitors to websites are called traffic. Now, most tutors will work locally and use the website to direct people to for further information so you don't need to worry about getting other traffic to your site. If, however, you are selling materials, have a lot of local competition or willing to work as a distance tutor via email then you do need to think about this. The process of designing your site for traffic is called web site optimisation and there are lots of books and websites about it.

Website optimisation tips:

✓ Get other sites to link into your site, search engines follow links from other sites to yours and will rate yours higher if you have lots of good quality links to it.

✓ Have lots of text based information. Search engines base their algorithms on the information you have not the pictures.

✓ Make sure you have the keywords people would use to find your site like your home town, county, the topics you tutor in and your name.

✓ You could use google adwords but make sure you make the ad very specific to your area and that you put a maximum daily spend on the ad or you could start to run up large bills.

Fees and Potential Income

With regard to tuition the second most frequently asked question is **'how much should I charge?'**

This is always a difficult one to answer and one that I gave great deal of thought to when I began tutoring over 15 years ago. One way to gauge the right amount is to do a bit of secret shopper research - phone the other people advertising in your local paper (with a particular problem in mind). Find out what they charge per hour and whether they have any space (if they are all full with waiting lists what a brilliant opportunity for you!) If you don't want to be deceptive why not just be honest and explain what you're doing - the worst they can do is put the phone down. If you don't want to ring your direct competitors why not try those a little further afield but make sure their area has similar households to your local ones.

If you charge too little, for example £10 for one hour's tuition, surprisingly you will not get a great deal of work. It is a common misconception that the cheaper your fees the more popular your service will be. If you go to the other extreme of charging too much however i.e. well over £30, you will obviously not attract many clients unless you are based in London. I think you need to start at a minimum of £19 per hour. It is important not to charge any less. After you establish yourself you can consider increasing your fee to £24 to £28 depending on your location. In London, as one would expect, it is not uncommon for a fee of £30 (and above) per hour to be charged. I live in the North of England (in the Rossendale Valley to be precise) where prices need to reflect the local economy.

The important thing is not to feel guilty when you start by charging £19 or more. You are providing a professional service, satisfying a need and, hopefully, giving value for money. If you think it is too much you will feel embarrassed when taking the money. You must not. You must feel confident and comfortable with your fee and tell yourself you are well worth it – even on your first visit to your first client.

If you are in doubt – try getting a plumber, electrician or TV repairman out for less than £25 per hour or ask your local garage mechanic what he charges per hour.

Now we come to the question do you want to do this part time or go for it as a full time job? Many people I have trained over the years have already got a full time job and need a little more income. This is something you can try while keeping your present job, as tutor can only be done between 4pm and 9pm in the evenings. I am acquainted with 56 year old lady who is perfectly happy to tutor just one child per night Monday to Friday. At £20 per hour (lesson) she earns £100 per week, or £450 per month. This extra money pays for her mortgage and she is perfectly content with this. You can see that if she tutored two children each night her income would be £900 per month. This is now going to be seriously useful money.

Then, there is the other extreme, where it is possible to tutor five children per night Monday to Friday and maybe a couple on a Saturday or Sunday morning. This results in 27 x £20 = £540 per week which equates to a gross salary of £25 920 per year (allowing for four weeks holiday). This is only charging £20 per hour and does not count time available to you during the day. I once trained a policeman who had become disillusioned with his job. He gave up the force after only 13 weeks and turned to tuition full time. He is now earning more by only working in the evenings than he did in the police force and, more importantly, is far happier and free from stress.

Always remember that theoretically you are free during the day, but the more children you have to tutor the more planning and preparation you will have to do during the day and/or at weekends. When assessing your income the only overhead of note is petrol or maybe public transport costs. Yes, it is possible to be a tutor without a car.

> **Case study:**
>
> I recently trained a lady in Blackpool, who had no access to the car during the evenings, as her husband needed it for his job. She built up a few clients on a housing estate two miles from her home. She left home at 3.30pm in a taxi, travelled to her first client for a 4pm appointment, later tutoring three more children within walking distance. She completed her last lesson at 8.30pm and was home before 9pm. Total income £80, total cost of taxis £5 each way. The lady did this just two evenings a week, which made her over £600 per month. If she'd wanted to earn even more money she could have travelled by bus – after all, she only had a briefcase to carry.

Possible overheads:

➢ Books - but these are a once only acquisition.

➢ Stationery - only a negligible ongoing cost – paper, pens, folders, etc. (See the back of the book for a comprehensive list of stationery requirements.)

➢ Travel - make sure your car insurance covers business travel, many companies include it automatically but others exclude it so you need to check your policy.

➢ Tax - if your total income goes over the personal allowance you will have to pay income tax.

If you and your spouse are on your own and have no ties, having brought up your children, and perhaps are in your 50s or 60s (in my opinion the ideal age to take up a career as a private tutor) why not consider both becoming tutors. I have in the past trained someone only to find that their husband or wife has also shown an interest in becoming a tutor.

Case study:

For example, a short while ago in Leighton Buzzard a 57 year old lady began by tutoring the 7 to 9 years age group in basic mathematics and English and built up quite a few clients per week. She was increasingly being asked if she could help secondary school children of 13 years and above but she did not feel her mathematics was strong enough. Her husband, aged 61 years (an ex-engineer) saw her frustration in declining these inquiries and decided he would take them on. After only six months she was tutoring 15 to 17 primary school children per week and her husband was tutoring 10 secondary school children per week. I shall leave you to check the mathematics but they are currently enjoying a joint income of over £1700 per month (charging £17 per hour each). They are both pulling in the same direction (still only working part-time) and have created a profitable interest together, leading into their retirement.

Tax and record keeping

You have a responsibility to inform the Inland Revenue that you are working as self employed even if you do not expect to go over the personal allowance. Just contact www.hmrc.gov.uk or ring 0845 915 4515 for advice.

Keep all receipts related to your work, including computers, books and stationery. Maintain an accurate and regular record of all payments received. Keep an accurate note of your mileage or other travel costs. The reason for this is that you can offset your expenses against your income to minimise the tax you need to pay. You shouldn't need an accountant as the self assessment form is very, very easy to fill in but you do need to watch the return dates or you can get fined.

You should also find out whether you need to register with the data protection people as you are going to be keeping details of your clients. This costs very little, see www.ico.gov.uk.

Make sure you save about 20% of your income to pay your tax bill. You also need to contact national insurance to determine whether you need to make any contributions on an on-going basis.

Do I need to have a limited company?

No, and it usually is not a good idea unless you are either going to earn over £50 000, where you start to make tax savings, or employ other people as it adds lots of extra administration and would mean you'd need to pay around £1000 for an accountant. It is a nice idea to name your business, which you can as a sole trader. It also makes it easier to get a business bank account if you have a trading name. If you are not limited you must not use the word limited or Ltd. in your company name.

Do I need insurance?

You definitely need to check your car policy includes business use and if it doesn't arrange the extra cover (some companies include it as standard so check your policy). With regards to further insurance such as professional indemnity and liability it is not a legal requirement but you may wish to investigate it yourself.

Exercise:

How many nights a week do you want to work?

....

How many tutees a night could you see? (Remember you need time to say goodbye and time to travel.)

....

If you charged £20 per hour and had 5 weeks holiday a year how much could you earn?

....

[See the page 139 for ideas on record keeping]

How much you can earn is up to you but do be warned – if you start off small this is something that will take off – perhaps quicker than you realise.

Handling the Initial Response

Your first call or email might frighten you; I remember mine did. Try to relax, however, and be prepared and professional. You may wonder, deep down, if anyone will ever reply to your advert but be assured they will – and when they do, don't panic. On the other hand, don't be discouraged if replies are not immediately forthcoming; you would be surprised how many people tear out and save adverts for long periods of time until they require the services on offer.

Keep a script next to the phone, but don't read directly from it. Practise your responses in advance and use the script only as a prompt. This is important as you will probably be nervous when your first potential clients call and could easily forget to ask obvious and important questions. It is a good idea to have a batch of the blank forms I have designed (a suggested sheet headed 'Student Details' can be found at the back of the book) by the phone in readiness. These will ensure you take down the address and telephone number of the people who are calling. Yes, I know this sounds obvious, but if you are a little nervous and become involved in conversation about their child you could easily put the phone down without asking for their address – how would you then get to their home? I have been guilty of this myself in the past. Believe me, it is not very professional to have to ring back and ask where your caller lives.

Be cool and calm on the phone but not too business like. Ask as much as you can about the child – parents love to talk about their children and their answers will give you time to listen rather than talk. Ask where they heard about you – this is important as you need to know which form of advertisements – and the areas – that are producing the best results for you. Ask the name of the child's school, their age, year in school and key stage and/or level (parents may not know the latter). You will find the biggest problem in schools and with children of all ages is numeracy or maths, followed by literacy or English. Over 75% of the children I have on my books at any one time require help with maths. Don't worry, the problems nearly always lie with the basics, even in the case of older children. Ask what the problem is over the phone but don't worry about defining specific subject areas, the parents will usually tell you they are behind in maths generally anyway.

Pretend you are putting the phone down and finding your diary to see what free appointments you have remaining and when you can fit them in. Yes, I know we're talking about your very first clients but don't let the parents know they are the first to contact you. Remember to create a professional image right from the start. Do not visit them immediately or the next day, even though you will be eager to get out there and begin your work. Say, for example, 'How does next Thursday at 6pm sound?' You will need time to prepare, get over the shock, think clearly and calm down.

Keep a supply of blank forms handy by your phone. At the back of the book you'll find a version of the form to copy or you can download any of the forms from the private tutoring section of www.uolearn.com

Student Details	
Name of student:	
Parents' names:	
Contact source:	
Address and Directions:	Tel:
	Email:
School:	Ages & D.O.B.
Year:	Key stage level:
Reason for calling:	
Weaknesses and Problems:	
Initial assessment date and time:	

Ask if you may see the child's reports and current or past work when you arrive. In my opinion most school reports are not worth the paper they are written on and usually should be taken with a 'pinch of salt'. They might, however, just give you a clue or insight into what the problems may be – and you will sound professional in expressing an interest in seeing them. Emphasise the following points:

➢ That you will visit them. (We will discuss this in detail later.) Many parents assume they bring the child to you. In fact, many tutors do work this way – so you are at an immediate advantage over any competition.

➢ You only do one-to-one intensive tuition concentrating on weaknesses. Don't be tempted to do two children at once – again, this will be discussed later in detail.

➢ You set homework every visit for the following week. This pleases and impresses parents.

➢ You do an assessment of the child on the first visit that may run over one hour, as you will need to chat with the parents at the end. Only charge your hourly fee, however – this impresses parents as they are getting a little extra for nothing.

If you are challenged about being 'qualified' then ensure you tell them anything relevant from your experiences – but read again the 'A Question of Qualifications' section to give you confidence. (The qualification question rarely comes up anyway.)

Lastly and most importantly tell the parents not to worry – give them confidence from day one that you will make an immediate improvement. Yes, I know it sounds like a tall order but you must say this (I will discuss why in detail in 'How to Get an Immediate Improvement' and you will then realise how simple it is).

Exercise:

Make a list of the 6 things you think a parent will ask you - what will your answer be?

....

....

....

....

....

....

....

....

....

What are the 6 most important things you need to ask the person who rings to enquire about your services?

....

....

....

....

....

....

....

....

....

....

....

Planning a Timetable

This can be quite a challenge when you suddenly become busier... and you will. At first you will travel virtually anywhere and this is OK. You are not going to refuse anyone. It is, however, best to be sensible and maybe decide how far you are prepared to travel from your home and out of the area.

Case study:

I remember my very first client (a 14 year old girl) many years ago lived in a small village approximately six to seven miles from my home. I didn't think twice about going that far (now I couldn't do it) and arranged to visit every Tuesday at 4pm. After only three weekly visits she and her parents recommended me to her friend, who was in the same class at the same school and also struggling with maths. I then arranged to visit her friend at 5:10pm on the same night as she only lived around the corner from the girl. After a further month of helping these two girls with noticeable success a mutual friend of them both rang me, also wanting help with her maths. Now, of course, I was driving to this village and coming home with £45 at 7:30pm for three hours' work and it was only costing me a couple of pounds worth of petrol. During this time I also picked up clients more local to me and I was starting to get organised visiting different areas on different evenings.

If you do take on a child some distance away, rather than refuse them, take plenty of your leaflets with you and target shops and venues near the client's house on one of your visits. Ensure also that the child's parents have some of your leaflets and make it known you are looking for more clients in their area, even offering them a discount or free lesson if they successfully recommend you.

As you plan your timetable ensure that you try to visit the younger children earlier or first, leaving the older ones until later in the evening. It sounds obvious but years 3-5 (7-10 year olds) tend to respond better before 7:30 pm, whereas 15 year olds studying for GCSEs are fine up until 9:30 pm and perhaps beyond. I currently visit five on some evenings (which is about the maximum) starting at 3:45 – 4:45 pm with my younger children and tutoring up to 8:30 – 9:30 pm for my last one; a year 11 student needing help for forthcoming GCSEs.

At first you may find you are going back on yourself along the same route or road. This, unfortunately, may have to be done in order to visit the younger children first and older ones last.

It is important, too, that you take into account any out of school activities that many children participate in these days – Brownies, football, judo, swimming, dancing and music lessons, etc. Do not (unless absolutely necessary) let a parent cancel a child's activity because they think your tuition is more important. In essence your visit is more important but it is also essential that children are encouraged in any other outside activities to develop their confidence, status and social skills. Imagine, too, how difficult it would be to motivate a ten year old, keen footballer in an hour of mathematics tuition, when he has had to sacrifice his training night. You would be off to a bad start in trying to win the child over and getting through to him will always be difficult.

When planning your visits take into account well known traffic bottle necks in your area as you will be travelling around at rush hour time in most areas (5pm- 6pm). Watch out for unexpected road works and temporary traffic lights. It is a good idea to sometimes try a route out first. Take a dummy run and look out for short cuts you could use en route to avoid being held up.

You need to allow five or ten minutes in addition to travelling time between clients' homes. Sometimes parents like to chat about their child at the end of a lesson or on your way out and, being professional, you can't just quickly walk out at the end of a session. Obviously politely say, 'I must get off to my next child.' If you find it difficult to break the conversation. You must, however, be strict – only give one hour, even if you haven't got a next client to go to.

If you get into the habit of letting certain clients 'keep you' past the hour knowing you are free after the lesson, one day you may have someone to visit next and it will appear impolite if you leave quicker than usual and don't have time to chat.

At the end of this book is a suggested copy of a sample timetable, which I use. I think it is useful to have two weeks on view so that you can double-check if 'same time next week' is OK or if your client has a problem – a dental appointment or holiday, etc., which you can immediately write in the correct slot.

Lastly but most importantly I think it is a good idea to leave a copy of your timetable at home with your spouse or partner, next to the phone. Obviously add telephone numbers and parents' names to the form. This 'insurance copy' will be useful if you break down and cannot get through to the client; simply ring home and your partner can do this for you whilst you are tied up trying to fix the car or waiting for the RAC or AA. There could be a situation where your second client of the evening has been taken ill suddenly and the parents are unable to contact you before you leave home. Your partner could ring through to your first client and speak to you or leave a message. In any emergency it is always common sense to inform your spouse or someone at home as to where you are.

First Visit and Assessment

Having recovered from your first telephone call response, the nerves might return when you visit the house and meet the parents and child for the first time. Try to keep calm, cool and professional, as first impressions are vital. Be on time, never late, but not too early either. If you are not sure where you are going take a dummy run days before, or leave in plenty of time and kill time sitting in the car away from the home if you find the location quicker than you had anticipated. If you have made the appointment for 6pm do not ring the doorbell until five to six at the earliest. Don't forget, the parents might be a little nervous too or may have rushed back from somewhere to be on time, and would not appreciate you arriving earlier than expected.

When you enter the house the parent(s) will tend to monopolise you, talking 'ten to the dozen' about anything and everything. Don't forget the purpose of your visit – the child – who will be peeping around the parents trying to get a look at the 'ogre' who has come to do maths with them. Ensure you introduce yourself (if the parents haven't already done so) to the child as quickly as possible. Pass the time of day or just talk to them at the expense of politely ignoring the parents; or at worst try to include them in the conversation.

Initial assessment	
Name of student:	
Date and time:	
Likes best:	Dislikes most:
Present school report comments:	
Reasoning:	Personality and first impressions:
Spelling:	
Alphabet:	
Maths:	
Tables:	Weakness from assessment:
Shapes:	
Fractions:	
GCSE level and assessment:	
Suggested tutoring period:	
Comments:	

There are some forms at the end of the books that you can copy, they can also be downloaded from the website, www.uolearn.com. Here are a couple of examples of filed in forms.

Initial assessment	
Name of student: Adam Fletcher	
Date and time: Monday 7th April, 6.30	
Likes best: Science and Art	**Dislikes most:** Maths
Present school report comments: Tries hard, put off by written work, helpful in class	
Reasoning: Fair	**Personality and first impressions:** Glasses, bubbly
Spelling: Good (15/20)	Small for age, red hair
	Not afraid to ask if stuck
Alphabet:	Well mannered
	Took to me OK after 1/2 hour
Maths: Poor on problems	
Tables: Stuck on 7,8 and 9	**Weakness from assessment:** Doesn't understand fractions properly
Shapes: Recognised most	Makes careless mistakes when carrying numbers
Fractions: Poor - needs help	Tables fair but weak on some
GCSE level and assessment:	English good but needs help in writing stories
Suggested tutoring period: Monday 4-5 or Friday 6-7	
Comments Gym club Weds, swimming Thurs	

Initial assessment

Student record			
Name of student:			
Adam Fletcher			
Initial assessment date and time:			
Monday 7th April 6.30			
Lesson time and date	Work done in hour	Homework	Comments
Mon 7th April 4.00	Assessment, got thru 8 - all marked	Punctuation sheet	Fractions need urgent attention
Mon 14th April 4.00	Went over all assessment tests	Test corrections	spotted weakness in telling time
Mon 21st April 4.00	Start fractions. Basics - put in order, cancelling down	Basic fractions	Good session
Mon 28th April 4.00	Try harder fractions Improper, mixed numbers etc	Comprehension. story for holidays	Tried English for a change over the holiday
Mon 5th May 4.00	Holiday		24 hour clock ASAP
Mon 12th April 4.00	Perform 8x table (9x if time allows)	Learn 8x table	Took a while to settle after holiday

Complete student record.

You will have some idea why you have been asked to help but do not believe too much of what the teachers have said (via reports) or, in fact, the parents. Find out for yourself from the child. There will usually be a 'quiet' place (preferably with a table) where you and the child can sit reasonably closely together. Some younger children who are perhaps nervous or a little shy may benefit from the parents' suggestion of sitting with them. If this happens (which is quite rare) then agree to it but don't let it put you off and make it clear that 'Mum or Dad must be quiet and not interfere or interrupt.' Usually the child cannot wait to have you to his or herself and will promptly insist mum or dad disappears to the next room.

Before you start any work or written assessment take ten minutes to talk to the child. Break the ice by asking them about what they like best and hate most at school. Say you are going to visit regularly to make them better at maths/English so they can impress their teacher and their friends and make mum and dad happy too.

You can then start to give them an assortment of sheets on maths and/or English. Tell them it doesn't matter if they get them right or wrong and not to think of them as tests or exams – say, 'They are only for me to get to know what you can or cannot do.' Pretend to make notes on your own form. You will need to do this anyway but watch the child closely out of the corner of your eye and monitor how they answer questions, their speed, whether they ask you constantly for help, their concentration level, if they skip too quickly without giving questions much thought, if they understand the sums or spellings, etc. If you find the child struggling, give them an easier sheet next, or, if they complete a sheet easily and quickly choose a harder one next. It doesn't matter how many they get through in forty-five minutes to one hour but try to give them an assortment so you can discover as much as you can about the child's different abilities. You will see at the end of this chapter a few sample tests I take with me but you can easily devise some of your own. You may order various packs of these masters to photocopy – details at the back of the book.

Do not be surprised to find weaknesses you were not expecting – i.e. spelling when you thought the problem was mathematics. Mark the tests quickly as the child completes them so you have a rough idea of what they find a problem – and you can show the parents what they have done at the end of the hour.

Make extensive notes on your form regarding your first impressions of the child and weaknesses you have found, etc. Although it is difficult on first meeting to assess the child completely in an hour you will have a good idea of what is needed by the end of the assessment. Obviously with experience you will assess each child easier and quicker. See the completed sample forms in this section. They will illustrate the type of information and comments I note on the first visit. There is also a blank form for you to photocopy at the back of the book, if you so wish.

After 45 to 60 minutes, on completion of a few tests, praise the child for their help and concentration, before you talk to their mum and dad and again just before you leave the house. When you talk to the parents (preferably without the child present) explain what the child has done and what you have found. Tell them not to worry because you can put things right. Ask if you can take home any school reports to photocopy and study together with statements and I.E.P.'s (more about statemented children in the section on 'Statemented and Special Needs Children'.) You may not place much credence on their content but it gives you more time to read them and study them at home before your next visit.

You may think what needs putting right with the child is unbelievably simple and it probably is, but things as basic as fractions, decimals or percentages may be beyond the understanding and ability of the average parent who may also be a product of poor schooling. This is where your help is invaluable, as the parents may have no way, except through you to help their child. Sad, but unfortunately true.

Explain how your tuition works i.e. a weekly visit for one hour at a time to suit you all. Appreciate the importance of working around brownies, cubs, judo, swimming, ballet, etc., and the many other activities children participate in. As stated previously,

Example assessment sheets

Measure the shapes below and write against each side the correct length in both centimetres and millimetres

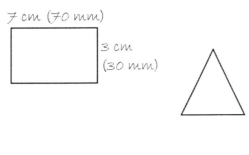

7 cm (70 mm)

3 cm
(30 mm)

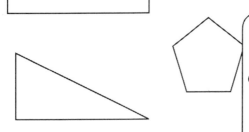

Circle the sum, the answer to which matches the large number at the top of each block. The first one is done for you.

17
18 + 2
19 - 2
7 + 2
5 + 10

18
5 + 15
13 - 7
2 + 17
15 + 3

13
19 - 6
5 + 13
13 - 9
10 + 5

14
18 + 1
17 - 3
9 + 11
13 - 2

12
14 + 6
13 - 1
12 + 7
8 + 5

19
17 + 2
16 - 3
5 + 11
19 - 6

10
5 + 10
17 - 9
19 - 9
18 + 1

15
10 + 7
9 + 6
13 - 7
16 + 3

11
16 + 3
10 + 5
19 - 3
18 - 7

it is important that they, as much as possible, keep these on; as trying to motivate them, knowing they have given up a favourite activity will be difficult. Suggest to the child that they get a folder in which to keep some of the work done with you. Encourage them to also keep a small notebook in which to write down anything that is worrying them at school, no matter how insignificant this may appear to you. Many children today are frightened to ask the teacher at school if they cannot understand something – some even too shy to put their hand up. The pace and speed of trying to cover all the National Curriculum (especially in primary schools) does not allow time for backtracking or repeating points that are not readily understood. If a child knows he or she can ask you in the comfort of their own home when you come round you will quickly gain their confidence. Girls are usually better organised and not as lazy – they also love the 'secrecy' aspect of this.

Whilst at the house don't forget to pass the time of day with and acknowledge other brothers or sisters. This is vital as they could be feeling jealous or left out and many also want or need to be tutored. Remember their names and talk to them at every opportunity – they could be your next clients.

Make a point also of remembering and using the first names of parents – add them to your forms so you will not forget them. Ensure you remember their names for your next visit as this will create a better atmosphere and relationship and impress them. Always leave parents confident and enthusiastic, tell them they can phone you at any time if they or their child have a problem, either at school or with homework. A week is a long time in a child's school life. Lots can happen, and parents will feel happier knowing they can contact you between visits. Many tuition agencies or tutors only answer the phone in office hours, which is frustrating when a parent needs to speak to you in the evening.

Above all, when you leave the client's home on your first visit ensure the child is enthusiastic and the parents are left with the peace of mind that your help will make a difference. This will give you a wonderful feeling – one of many you will come to savour.

Exercise:

List 3 important points to mention to the child on your first visit.

....

....

....

....

....

....

List 3 things to discuss with the parents on your assessment visit.

....

....

....

....

....

....

Preparation

Being organised comes naturally to some people, unfortunately not to us all. This will probably not matter if you have only three or four children to tutor but, as your business grows rapidly (which it will), beware! Luckily I am naturally organised, which is just as well. I currently have twenty three clients on my list with a waiting list of a further five. Fortunately I have an office at home in which I can work quite comfortably surrounded by files, trays and books. You need to allocate a corner of the lounge or bedroom until your business grows but, as I have warned, I have seen many a conservatory or spare room gradually turn into an office. Partners may not be too pleased.

The essentials (which are detailed at the back of the book) are a briefcase, stationery, books you will gradually accumulate, and wallet files. Open a file for each child and use separate trays for each day to hold them in. You will need additional trays for loose sheets (keep mathematics and English separate), work to be marked, infants, older children, GCSE work, exam and test papers, etc. Your system is very much up to you, and a matter of what you feel comfortable with.

Your briefcase (the contents of which are detailed at the back of the book) will be taken into every home and must contain a folder/file with assorted spare work sheets for all age groups. You will also obviously take the child's folder with all your information on that child inside, plus the work you have planned for that lesson, with you.

> "Seventy five percent of my entire client base from six to sixteen years old requires mathematics tuition."

Always, always remember to prepare for the lesson before you arrive and always prepare more than enough work just in case they whiz through things quickly. For this eventuality you must always carry a folder with spare worksheets in your briefcase. It will be embarrassing for you to have finished the hour's work you had planned in half an hour with a child and to be left panicking for the remainder of the lesson.

Ensure you have last week's homework marked before you visit the child. They will look forward to discovering how many marks they have achieved – remember when you were at school how you felt when the teacher hadn't yet marked a homework you were dying to get back. At worst take the homework back to the home with you unmarked and let the child mark it as you read out the answers. Children love to do this.

Most people I have trained over the years have decided to tutor only primary school children up to year 6 (11 years old). This is fine – the work is obviously easier and it is by far the biggest market requiring home tuition. Eighty percent of my clients at any one time are in junior school. Whilst we are on the subject of statistics, seventy five percent of my entire client base from six to sixteen years old requires mathematics tuition, by far the biggest fear of most children and their parents.

As you become involved in home tuition consider offering other subjects to help children if you have experience in them – for example, science, French, history, music or I.T. Clients will not 'beat a path to your door' for these subjects (mathematics being the most popular) but you would be foolish not to mention them to parents or include them in your advertisements.

You will often find yourself in W.H.Smith looking for mathematics and English books, but only buy the ones you feel comfortable with and can understand yourself. (Preferably with answers provided for speed.) Different books treat topics differently (such as fractions) so choose the ones you like best. I tend to favour the now 'old fashioned' methods that I was taught, and this is where you can score over schools where newer, modern methods, especially in mathematics, have left children and parents utterly confused.

As you become more confident and aware of the methods children respond to best, begin to design and write out your own work sheets. Many of the exercises and sheets that I designed are based on examples that I found in books. Beware, however, of infringing copyrights. Fortunately many educational books allow you to photocopy their pages as long as you use them for children to work from. At the end of this book you have the opportunity to send for any of my worksheets which I permit you to freely photocopy or take ideas from and to redesign to suit yourself without infringing any copyright.

Above are some of the books you can find in a typical book shop. Details of the main publishers are at the back of the book. You can even pick some of them up at the cheaper book shops that sell remaindered books.

If you buy workbooks, rather than actually writing in them, photocopy any relevant pages so you can use the examples with every child. If you design your own worksheets keep one as a master in good condition and run a few copies off so you always have spares. Label and file your masters in age or school year ability, keeping different topics in separate files. As you grow busier this will help you to find a specific worksheet or example quickly. The whole process is made very much easier if you have access to a PC as you can print copies as you require them.

Constantly add to and update your information. New methods (particularly in mathematics) will be brought to your attention by the children themselves. Ask if you can borrow (in order to photocopy) any tests or homework that the child may have brought home from school to show you or ask for your help. You may be able to use the examples with other children you have on your books of similar age or ability.

In conclusion, ensure you do all the preparation necessary before you visit your client.

Exercise:

Are you an organised person?

Think of 3 ways to help make sure you are ready for your tutorials.

....

....

....

Professionalism

One of the biggest advantages I have over other private home tutors is the fact that I visit the client, not vice versa. Many parents assume, when they initially enquire, that they have to bring their child to you. This presents many disadvantages for the client and, being professional, as you must always be, you do not want your client to experience ANY disadvantages when dealing with you.

Imagine if you were a parent travelling to a tutor... you would have to get your child ready, set off in good time in order to find the address and perhaps have to drive to the other side of town in what could be inclement weather. If you are a single parent you might even have to 'drag' another child out on the journey or arrange for a babysitter or journey via your parents' home in order to leave the other child with its grandparents. There is so much hassle a tutor-visiting client may have to go through. Then consider the cost of petrol... and what happens when the parent arrives at the tutor's... how do they kill an hour? This routine would soon prove irksome for parents and children alike and result in you losing a client.

A child works better in the comfort of its own home with the assurance of knowing mum and dad are in the next room. This is especially important in today's environment of sexual innuendoes when a child is left with an adult 'stranger'.

I am obsessed by punctuality. I feel it is vital. If you are unavoidably going to be late inform the client out of courtesy. As previously mentioned, check the route and shortcuts first to ensure you are on time. Always dress smartly, never too casual. I suppose I'm showing my old fashioned ways again but I always like to wear a tie (this does not apply, of course, to female tutors!). I think a tie presents a professional image whilst always looking smart. It's up to you and will depend on your age, upbringing and sex. Do not smoke at a client's home, even if you are offered a cigarette from parents who are smoking. If you must smoke in your own car between clients ensure you always keep mints in the car or a spray to hide the objectionable smell. There is nothing worse than entering a non-smoking house smelling of cigarettes. It is very off-putting to children who have to sit close to you during the hour's lesson. Out of the twenty-three houses I visit during a week there are only two homes in which parents smoke. Thankfully the trend is dying out.

Ask parents regularly how their child is progressing at school and always ask the child if they have any problems with their lessons in school. Read reports from school and ask to photocopy them if you wish, as the information may be useful in future. Look at any certificates or awards the child may have received and praise them lavishly for earning them, telling them to be proud of their achievements.

Be prepared to drop the planned lesson immediately. A child may have come home from school that day with a problem or homework that cannot wait. To go over this work there and then is priceless to the child; and to the parents too if they have been unable to help. This is where the flexibility of private home tuition is invaluable. Schools have to follow pre-planned lessons and cannot immediately change a lesson plan for one or two children. You can.

If parents are about to go to their child's parents' evening at school knowing they may be embarrassed by their offspring's underachievement, offer to photocopy some of the better work they have done with you. This will prove to schoolteachers that the child is capable of producing satisfactory work, albeit at home, and, more importantly, give the parents and child confidence.

If you have a really good lesson when everything goes to plan and you and the child are in good form, when you have left the house write down the features that made it successful – the timing and presentation, etc. This allows you to repeat the performance, maybe with a few modifications. Equally, if you have had a bad lesson where nothing seemed to go right, ask yourself where you went wrong, how you could improve on it and make notes of what you would never do again. As a course of habit always makes notes, good or bad, at the house there and then; if you do not you will forget as soon as you visit the next child or return home.

Every child is different and requires a different approach to motivate them and help them understand what you are doing with them. Your own sense of humour will dictate to what degree you have a laugh and a joke with them on each visit. If your personality is a bit dry and serious then try to lighten up. The children will appreciate it, I can assure you. They have had a 'dry' and 'serious' day at school. Remember, do not try to be like a teacher.

Ensure they know you are fallible too; make little mistakes on purpose and congratulate them for spotting those mistakes and correcting you. They will love this. This is all part of gaining a child's confidence and winning them over. As you develop a rapport with a child, be careful. Teachers will sometimes appear jealous and ridicule you through the parents, especially if the child does their best work for you whilst not trying too hard at school. Do not worry too much about this; it is not really your problem. Your confidence will grow with each visit and you will not believe how easy tuition becomes once you have won over the child and parents. They will look forward to your next visit, which will give you a satisfied feeling, knowing you are doing something important and worthwhile and getting paid for it.

Every child is different, and so are parents. Some are more interested than others in what you are doing. Some want to know what you have done at the end of every lesson, but most parents just let you get on with it. Sometimes I don't see a parent – the child answers the door, we sit and do the one-hour lesson, and the money is left on the table for me. When the family gets to know you better after a few weeks you will be trusted and usually left on your own. Beware, however, of a parent wanting to sit in on every lesson. On the first visit it may be necessary if you have a particularly shy, younger child, but you have to quickly win this child over so mum and dad do not have to sit with you. It is distracting for the child and for you, and most parents understand this. I tutor one 14-year-old girl client whose mother always asks if it would be alright for her to sit in on the lesson. I make an exception as long as she does not interfere or distract her daughter. Her daughter is not put off and doesn't mind mum's presence. Her mum says it is the 'highlight' of her week and she learns more about maths than she ever did in school.

Be professional but be yourself; stamp your personality on the child and family. Pay attention to brothers and sisters – even leave them a worksheet if they show any interest- as I mentioned earlier they will probably be your next clients. Always have plenty of leaflets and cards handy to leave a satisfied parent; they will always know other parents and their children.

Remember, you are just as important (probably more so) as a teacher in a child's life. You are a friend, a counsellor, a listener and a sounding board for them. You will find yourself being asked an assortment of questions and queries, not only from the child but from the parents, too.

Until you become experienced you will not realise how quickly some children can get through work. Always have something else ready just in case. On the other hand, if you do not finish all the work you had planned for the hour, don't worry. If the lesson is going well and the child is understanding what you are doing and you are enjoying it, then it does not matter if you finish or not; remember they can always finish it off for homework.

It is vital that you do not rush the lesson. Many people I have trained rang me in the early days to say they felt guilty if they did not cram the whole hour with activity and work. They felt they were not giving value for money. On the contrary, you are giving value for money if you are winning the child over and getting through to them. You will only achieve this by going slowly.

It does not matter if it takes the full hour to do one or two long division sums as long as they know how to do them when you've gone. I cannot emphasise this enough. Please do not rush; go slowly.

Remember, this is where home tuition scores over the schools. They simply haven't got time to slow down and rarely have time for one-to-one lessons. Always keep an eye on the time so you can end comfortably in one hour. It is easy to forget how long you've been working when you become engrossed with a child. As you become more experienced you will develop an internal alarm clock that will remind you after fifty minutes to start to wind up the lesson and go over the homework without having to rush.

At the back of the book there is a blank form you can use to give parents feedback either on a weekly or monthly basis.

Finally, as you leave the house always remind the parents that they can ring you if they or their child has any problems before you return next week.

Exercise:

Many businesses have a code of conduct for their employees. This might cover things such as dress, punctuality, behaviour and recycling.

What's your code of conduct as a tutor?

....

....

....

....

....

How to get an Immediate Improvement

It is a fantastic feeling when you get an immediate improvement with a child, and not only for you – it also gives the child a confidence boost and impresses the parents. To facilitate an immediate improvement is relatively easy. You first find out what the child's biggest problem is and concentrate on this until they have solved it. This may be something quite minor to us (i.e. carrying numbers in subtraction sums) but obviously is a major problem for the child. Go right back to the basic problem and work through it slowly until the 'light starts to go on', repeating examples until the child understands it.

All children, even the bright ones, struggle with something they never understood at school in earlier years and, because there is never time in school to backtrack, the problem is forgotten. I meet many 15 year olds who are preparing for GCSEs and do not know how to do long multiplication and/or long division simply because they did not understand the concept when in year 6 at 10 years old.

The child may have a problem that is not academic. Many children are quite shy and withdrawn due to a variety of reasons. Overpowering teachers who shout in the classroom often affect shy or sensitive children who dare not put their hand up even when they know the answers.

You have to tread lightly with these children and slowly build up their confidence. Chat with them for the first ten minutes of a visit before you begin any work with them. They will 'come round' and begin to treat you as a friend, looking forward to your weekly visits. A large part of being a successful private home tutor concerns not just the academic side, but winning the child over and giving them confidence, talking with them about school in general or anything that they have done. Show an interest in them and not just their work – this is vitally important.

You could encounter the problem of bullying. It is quite widespread, especially verbal bullying between girls. Some schools acknowledge the problem, though many don't. You may be the first to discover a child is being bullied – they are quite likely to confide in a third party, telling you before telling their teachers or parents if you successfully win them over. You will then be faced with the dilemma of whether or not to say something to the parents, even though the child may beg you not to. Every situation is different and general advice is difficult but I would suggest you tell the parents discretely without breaking the child's confidence too much.

I have found that one excellent way of improving a child's confidence is to show them something they should not yet know. For example, a bright year 4 child (eight years old) could quite easily take on the technique of long multiplication or identifying different angles and maybe reading a protractor. This would not normally be covered until year 5 or even year 6.

Many school teachers would throw their arms up in horror at the suggestion but you are not visiting the child at home to please the teachers. It gives the child's confidence a terrific boost and the parents are always impressed.

> **Case study:**
>
> I once showed a year 6 boy, who was quite able and enthusiastic where maths was concerned, how to do Pythagoras one lesson before Christmas as a treat. It took me the full hour to explain what the theory was and how it worked and where it could be used. He was doing examples just before I left, showing his parent what he had learned. When he returned to school after the Christmas holiday he couldn't wait to demonstrate his new found knowledge to his maths teacher. Luckily, his teacher shared his excitement and praised him but pointed out that it would be another two years before he covered the subject in school. Who cares? The boy felt extremely pleased with himself, his friends felt a little envious and, most importantly, his confidence soared. He even bragged to his aunts and uncles about his new found skill repeatedly.

Being a little eccentric myself I tend to encourage children to think laterally and more logically. This is not really encouraged in schools today... excepting, perhaps, Grammar schools. I am a great believer in crosswords (one of the best and less boring ways of showing a child how to spell), IQ tests and verbal reasoning; the latter being part of the requirement for Grammar school admission. There is no harm, however, in doing verbal reasoning tests or examples with children in mainstream schools who have no intention of sitting the Grammar school entrance exams. It sharpens their logical thinking.

I find even bright Grammar school children are too focused and, whilst being brilliant at mathematics or I.T., they can exhibit very poor general knowledge skills. It is my opinion that computers should be limited to one hour a night for most children under thirteen years old. You will soon discover how difficult it can be to get through to a child who has spent three hours on a computer from coming home from school until you arrive. Sometimes it will be twenty to thirty minutes into the lesson before you get any sensible response. Computer-fatigued children resemble zombies with a vacant expression. Mention this to the parents and politely ask that the child does not spend much time on the computer before you arrive; it definitely makes a difference in communicating with a child.

Do not assume a child knows something. In other words, test the child yourself. Yes, a year 6 child (age ten years) should know the names of angles up to 360 degrees, i.e. acute, obtuse and reflex, but he may have been off school when they covered this and, as I repeat, there is no time for backtracking in school.

Talk to children as an adult and as a friend, never as a teacher. Use first name terms, not Sir or Mr. or Mrs. The exception to this can be within families from other cultures where adults are still addressed as Mr. or Mrs. Do you remember when all children were that respectful?

To get an immediate improvement with a child you need to 'switch them on', make them enthusiastic and excited about maths and English. You may ask, how can you make maths exciting. By presenting it in different and interesting ways. One night I knocked on the door of one of my regular year 5 girls. When she answered it I said, "Hello, how many minutes have you lived for?" I love doing this to children and after they get over the initial shock question they love it too. Solving this question took up the majority of the one hour lesson in working out the exact answer and made maths fun, even though we did a lot of adding and long multiplication.

Zany questions I ask children if I'm feeling eccentric are:

➢ How many minutes have you lived for?

➢ Can you swim in 100 litres of water?

➢ Can you fit the population of your town on 110 double decker buses?

➢ Can you write your full name and address on a square piece of paper measuring 1cm? (They tend to get annoyed when you ask why they did not use the other side too.)

➢ How many words can you make from your full name?

➢ How many vowels in the first names of all the members of your family?

➢ Would you drink enough in your life to fill a swimming pool?

➢ Could you eat one tonne of food in a year without getting too fat or too thin?

All questions are designed to make children think laterally (parents are more likely to show an interest in this type of homework question, too) whilst doing some mathematics and English. Make up some of your own, the possibilities are endless.

Exercise:

Think of 3 unusual questions to ask a child which could be related to maths.

....

....

....

....

....

....

One final point in getting an improvement is to spend time with the child on exam technique. Much of this is common sense to an adult generation but very little of this is mentioned in schools today, particularly now when at SATs and GCSE levels the exam papers clearly show the number of marks awarded for each question. Obviously the child needs to understand it is prudent to spend more time on the high mark questions and not to worry too much if they don't know an answer to a question where only one mark is awarded. Children need to feel confident enough to answer the last question first if they know it. This will put them in a more confident mood for the rest of the exam and ensure they start off quickly. Many children are taught to read all the questions first. I find this is not only a waste of valuable time but has a negative effect and can overwhelm the child, causing them to freeze and make them wonder how and where to start. Children, especially boys, are lethargic in self checking. Always encourage children to go through any questions they found difficult again if they have time at the end, even the ones they found easy to ensure they haven't made silly, careless mistakes.

Initially don't be too worried about getting through a vast amount of work with the child, thinking you have to give value for money. It is more important to be yourself, win the child over, and make a friend of them. Then an immediate improvement will be automatic.

Homework - 'to give or not to give?'

Whether to give homework or not is very much up to you as it is you who will have to mark it, usually in your own time at home, thus creating additional work. However, I strongly advise that you do leave the child homework on every visit, expecting it to be finished for your next visit in one week's time. Homework is very important for many reasons; firstly, not enough (if any) is given at school, despite the government's recommendations. It also gives the child a sense of importance and adds some seriousness to their private home tuition. Remember, you are only seeing the child for one hour per week so homework helps to keep the impetus and interest going in whatever you are helping them with. The parents will be impressed that the child is given homework, as many tutors don't bother.

Most children will be quite enthusiastic about the homework they are given by you, often giving it priority over their school homework. Beware if this happens as you do not want to upset the school. If you do not quite finish what you had planned for the one hour lesson then asking the child to complete it for homework is very useful rather than trying to finish the lesson off in a rush. Often children (especially the younger ones) will be eager to give you their homework as soon as you enter the house without you even having to ask for it. Encourage their enthusiasm by marking it with them before you start anything you have planned. Let them mark their own work whilst you read out the answers. Most younger children love to do this. Tell them not to worry about any wrong answers as you will go through them as soon as you have marked to the end. If the child's homework is perfect and 100% correct, praise them and ensure their parents know what a 'fantastic' piece of work they have done.

With younger children you can even give smiley face stickers to use on their work as a reward system. However, beware of unbelievable, unexpected high marks when you had a feeling the child didn't fully understand the subject the week before. This could be due to parents intervening or even doing the homework for them. Don't misunderstand me - it is important for parents to be encouraged to help and become involved in their child's work. This can be a tricky situation. It always amuses me that parents identify their child as having a big problem, pay for the home tuition, then ensure that the child always gets their homework 100% correct. If you find this happening regularly you need to tell the parents politely and gently not to help their child, or at least to identify and mark the questions which the child has needed help with.

There is absolutely no point in you thinking the child is doing well and has no problems if the homework is fully correct due to their parents' help. You need to know where the wrong answers are and why they are occurring so you can correct the child's weaknesses. If you find the child has many answers incorrect then always go through each question very slowly with them so they know exactly how and where they went wrong. If you wish do it there and then at the expense of the full hour's lesson you had planned. Do not feel guilty that you have spent the whole hour correcting homework. It is vital that you go through every wrong answer until the child knows where and how they went wrong. Schools never have time to do this on a one-to-one basis, and this is where private tuition is priceless.

If you feel embarrassed confronting parents about having helped with their child's homework, you can always add 'No Help' to the instructions you stick on the work. Ask the child to denote with an 'H' for help if they had to ask their mum or dad, but tell them they only get half a mark if this happens. Some of the more dedicated children will ensure parents don't intervene if it means they don't get a high mark from you. If you do suspect regular parental intervention ask the child at random how they arrived at their correct answer? If there is no sign of any working out in a mathematics question they may have just been told the answer or cheated by using a calculator. You will soon detect if you are having the 'wool pulled over your eyes'.

Although parents are keen to have their children appear clever, even to you, they are fooling you and, indirectly, their child for the wrong reasons. You need to know at all times the child's weaknesses and it is only by the child making errors (however embarrassing to them or their parents) that you will discover their problems.

Statemented and Special Needs Children

Statemented and special needs children are more evident in schools today than ever before. Their numbers more than doubled during the last 10 years and now they take up a staggering one third of the education budget. Despite this local authorities are still hopelessly under-funded when it comes to supplying the necessary support teachers that are needed in the classroom. The time allocated for each S.E.N. (Special Educational Needs) pupil is also never enough, fifteen hours a week being the maximum but usually anything from one and a half hours to two hours being the norm. I think that children with severe behavioural problems should not be integrated into the mainstream but attend a special school (of which there are far too few in the country).

Many classrooms are in chaos due to lack of discipline and constant disruption by a few pupils. I have worked in schools and seen first hand the frustration of teachers and S.S.A.s (Special Support Assistants). Disruptive children have no intention of doing any work, and 'infect' the children who are prepared to listen and work. My opinions or remedies are not suitable to print so I will confine myself to suggesting how you can tutor these children in their own home.

Underachievement and disruptive behaviour do not always go 'hand in hand.' Many children have problems with numeracy and/ or literacy and may even be dyslexic. There is a pleasant thirteen year old girl I visit once a week. She has been statemented as stage five (the severest). The different stages are listed at the end of this section. She has a reading age of between eight and nine years old and has short-term memory problems, but is enthusiastic and always approachable; in fact, a joy to help. Home tutoring has a distinct advantage with S.E.N. children as one-to-one is by far the best way of helping them. Schools cannot do this easily or for long enough periods and the child loses interest or cannot participate in any work with the rest of the class.

People will ask if you are 'qualified' to help S.E.N. children. You don't need any qualifications to be invited into their home to sit and help them with sums or reading. All you need is more patience than you would normally have and the ability to go right back to basics, possibly having to repeat or revise more work than you would with other children.

> **Case study:**
>
> When I first visited a little girl she was nine years old in a mainstream school and really couldn't do much of anything. The school had failed her and wasted four years of schooling. Her mother was desperate and asked me to start anywhere I liked with her; she had many problems. I began by teaching her to tell the time, which took me three months visiting one hour a week. This new found knowledge and confidence spilled over into other subjects, and she also improved in her spelling, reading and sums. Dyslexic children can be helped and encouraged to shine in many areas where they struggle in school.

The feeling of satisfaction from helping S.E.N. children at home is one of the best I have ever experienced. Schools may not have got through to them but knowing you will is a feeling to be cherished. This will give you confidence and the patience to take on other S.E.N. children. Generally, these children are getting a rough deal in school. Support assistants can only help each of them for a short time, as often there are many others in the same class requiring assistance. Most support assistants I know are mature people who have probably had more experience with children and their foibles than any number of recently qualified, non-parent teachers.

Stages in special needs registration

Stage 1: (special needs register)

The child's class teacher or form/year tutor has overall responsibility for gathering information about the child, providing help within the normal curriculum and monitoring and reviewing the child's progress. NB. At stage 1 no Individual Educational Plan is necessary.

Stage 2:

The school's S.E.N. co-ordinator takes the lead in co-ordinating the child's special educational provision, consulting the child's teachers, who remain responsible for working with the child in the classroom. The S.E.N. co-ordinator, working with the child's class teacher or form/year tutor and relevant curriculum specialists, should ensure that an individual education plan is drawn up. So far as possible the plan should build on the curriculum the child is following alongside fellow pupils and should make use of programmes, activities, materials and assessment techniques readily available to the child's class teachers. The plan should usually be implemented, at least in part, in the normal classroom setting. The S.E.N. co-ordinator should, therefore, ensure close liaison between all relevant teachers. The Code of Practice details the information that should be included in the individual education plan.

Stage 3:

As stage 2 above. This plan should be at implemented, at least in part, in the normal classroom setting. The S.E.N. co-ordinator should, therefore, ensure close liaison between all relevant teachers. The plan should ensure a co-ordinated cross-curricular and inter-disciplinary approach which takes due account of the child's previous difficulties.

"One in five children in our schools is now on a specials needs register, according to official statistics. In total more then 1.5 million pupils are classified as having "special educational needs.""

Stage 4:

This is the stage at which the child is referred to the local authority for statutory assessment. Amongst other things the referral requires – "written education plans at stages 2 and 3 indicating the approach adopted, the monitoring arrangements followed and the educational outcomes" and "reviews of each individual educational plan indicating decisions made as a result."

Stage 5:

The education authority has written a Statement of Educational Need for the child. The Statement identifies the child's special educational needs and special educational provision, which involves cross-curricular support and liaison between subject and support teacher. The Statement is a legal document and the school's governors may be held to account in a court of law if the special educational provision is not made. The Individual education plan is the instrument for liaising between the S.E.N. co-ordinator and subject specialists in meeting some of the requirements of the Code of Practice.

Exercise:

Find out what the following mean:

Dyslexia

....

....

Dyspraxia

....

....

Dyscalculia

....

....

The next page shows the type of individual education plan that a S.E.N. student might be given. This example was for a year 3 student.

Individual Education Plan

	Targets to be achieved	Achievement criteria	Possible resources/ technique	Possible class strategies	Ideas for support / assistant	Outcome
1	To read and spell all of the first 45 high frequency words	Accurate when tested at random when tested on three separate occasions.	Flashcards, games, worksheets, computer programs, tracking, tracing, cloze	Include the words in spelling activities and of the words and check that he reads/ spells them correctly in context.	Play games to encourage reading of the words and teach strategies for remembering spellings	
2	To read/spell c-v-c* words with vowel sounds a,e,i,o,u	Accurate when tested at random on three separate occasions.	Wooden / plastic letters, phonic workbooks, card games, computer programs, tracking, dictation.	Encourage him to write the sounds he hears in a spoken word and read the c-v-c words accurately.	Use multi-sensory methods for teaching c-v-c words. Set rhyming activities.	
3	To read and spell the next 11 of the year 1, 2 and 3 list of high frequency words	Accurate when tested at random when tested on three separate occasions.	Worksheets, flashcards, games, rainbow tracing, tracking, computer programs, words in context	Include words in spelling activities and check that he reads/ spells them correctly in context.	Play games to encourage reading of the words and teach strategies for remembering spellings.	

Parents/carer contribution: Help him to learn any spellings that are sent home. Make sure that words sent home are practised.

Student contribution: Practise reading the words. Practise the spellings, using strategies he has learnt. Try to apply spellings he has learnt to his own written work.

*c-v-c = consonant vowel clusters

Home Educating and the Law

Keeping your child at home to educate him or her is growing in popularity, and most parents are not aware that they are quite within their rights, and the law, so to do. The law states that every parent is legally bound to educate their children; sending them into school can be seen as one option but it is not compulsory. You may teach them at home for reasons that are your own business. The Local Education Authority may want to satisfy themselves that you are home educating but they have no right to legally intervene nor can they insist you follow the national curriculum or participate in any tests or exams.

Here are the facts:

Is it legal?

YES – It is the parent's duty to ensure that the child receives a proper education (Education Act 1996, Section 7; Education (Scotland) Act 1980, section 30; Education and Libraries (Northern Ireland) Order 1986, Article 45). Children of all ages can learn at home.

Do I have to inform the Local Education Authority?

NO – If your child has never been registered at a state school (or if you move to an area served by another LEA) you are not obliged to notify the LEA, although you may do so if you wish. If you are taking your child out of a state school in England or Wales the head teacher must remove the child's name from the register and inform the LEA.

YES – if you are withdrawing your child from a state school in Scotland or a special needs school.

Do I have to follow the National Curriculum?

NO – the law states the children may be educated according to the wishes of their parents (Education Act 1996, s 9; Education (Scotland) Act 1980, s 28; Education and libraries (NI) Order 1986 Art. 44)

Will my child have to take tests at the Key Stages?

NO – formal testing is not required. The Local Education Authority may ask for information at intervals in order to monitor your child's progress.

Can a child with a Statement of Special Educational Needs be educated at home?

YES – under S324 of the Education Act 1996 the Local Education Authority must make provision for the child's special educational needs unless the parent has made 'suitable arrangements' at home. Scotland and N. Ireland: similar provisions apply.

Is home education costly?

NO – you don't need a lot of expensive equipment. In some areas you can borrow equipment from the local education resource centre. Many single parents teach at home successfully on Income Support.

Can GCSEs be taken at home?

YES – some young people enter as private candidates or arrange for attendance at Further Education College to study for GCSEs. Others use correspondence courses.

Are children deprived of any social life?

No – in many areas home educators meet together regularly for social and educational activities and the children also attend clubs, classes, and sporting and leisure activities in the community. The children mix with people of all ages as well as their peers.

Do I have to be a teacher?

NO – enthusiasm and commitment are needed, not qualifications. Many parents learn alongside their children, so the whole family benefits from the experience.

Can you study Science at home?

YES – much of today's science is geared to real-life situations using equipment that is easily available at home. And even the most up-to-date school laboratory can't split the atom.

From http://direct.gov.uk/en/parents/schoolslearninganddevel-opment/choosingaschool/dg_4016124, Dec 09.

What's required of you

The facts about home education are:

➢ *you do not need to be a qualified teacher to educate your child at home*

➢ *your child is not obliged to follow the National Curriculum or take national tests, but as a parent you are required by law to ensure your child receives full-time education suitable to their age, ability and aptitude*

➢ *any special educational needs your child may have must be recognised*

➢ *you do not need special permission from a school or local authority to educate your child at home, but you do need to notify the school in writing if you're taking your child out of school*

➢ *you will need to notify the local authority if you are removing your child from a special school*

➢ *you do not need to observe school hours, days or terms*

➢ *you do not need to have a fixed timetable, nor give formal lessons*

➢ *there are no funds directly available from central government for parents who decide to educate their children at home*

➢ *some local authorities provide guidance for parents, including free National Curriculum materials*

The role of your local authority

Local authorities can make informal enquiries of parents who are educating their children at home to establish that a suitable education is being provided. If your local authority makes an informal enquiry, you can provide evidence your child is receiving an efficient and suitable education by:

➢ *writing a report*
➢ *providing samples of your child's work*
➢ *inviting a local authority representative to your home, with or without your child being present*
➢ *meeting a local authority representative outside the home, with or without your child being present (representatives have no automatic right of access to your home)*

If it appears to the local authority that a child is not receiving a suitable education, then it might serve a school attendance order.

Although you're not legally required to inform your local authority when you decide to educate your child at home, it is helpful if you do so. The only exception to this is where your child is attending a special school under arrangements made by the local authority. In this case additional permission is required from the authority before the child's name can be removed from the register.

If you are taking your child out of school to home educate them, you need to inform the school in writing. It's advisable, but not compulsory, to inform your local authority of any significant changes in your circumstance relevant to your child's education, like a change of address.

"Research from Australia shows that children taught by their parents at home are more than able to keep up with their conventionally educated peers. This is despite the fact that most lessons at home become more informal as time goes on."

There are many reasons why parents may consider not sending their child to school and educating at home. By far the biggest reason is because of bullying on a repetitive scale. Although schools do what they can it is extremely difficult to eradicate bullying (especially the verbal type) completely. Many parents are at their wits' end and are faced with the daily trauma of making their child go to school knowing the bullying will occur and continue. Keeping the child at home obviously solves this problem and brings peace of mind to both parent and child enabling the child to learn enthusiastically in the comfort of their own home.

Geographical concerns may be a reason for choosing to tutor a child at home, i.e. maybe no suitable school of parents' choice nearby. There may be no efficient bus service available and the family may not be able to afford taxis.

It could be that the child's personality makes them unsuitable for school environment; there are some children who have a phobia of school. A child may be a special needs child, either for behavioural or physical reasons, and the school may not be able to offer adequate support.

The reasons for wanting or indeed needing to home educate could only be temporary. For example, due to an accident or long illness the child could be off school for weeks or even months. The school has a duty to provide work at home for the child but most do not, so home education is the only alternative.

It is possible to keep a child at home even for two or three years then reinstate them at their original school. Some difficulty could be encountered with the head teacher (suggesting no places are available) especially if a child was withdrawn due to disagreement between the school and the parents. Parents are, however, within their rights to stop and start their child's schooling to suit the circumstances.

Many reasons for home educating are caused by the parent's disillusionment and frustration at the child's underachievement i.e. the child is becoming further and further behind in their work, his or her face doesn't fit, resulting in a personality clash with a teacher, etc. However, there is the other end of the spectrum – a parent with a very bright child. These children tend to get bored very quickly when they can do all the work that is given them – they need new and harder work to do, but the national curriculum and school system cannot really cater for them. This situation results in the child presenting behaviour problems and usually a clash between parents and teachers. It may be that the parents intend to send their bright child to a grammar school but the child is not old enough to sit the entrance examination yet. The parents may not yet be able to afford to send them to a private school where they would be stretched and encouraged. Home education is therefore an option to solve the problem. I have come across this situation several times.

There are many proven advantages to home education. Children invariably progress more rapidly, are better educated and display superior 'social graces' and manners than the average school child today does.

This is another plus private home tuition offers. Obviously most parents could not afford a private home tutor all day, every day but you could build up a client base where you could call on a child once or twice a week. You could set work, suggest ideas as to what they should be doing if at school and advise the parents on their child's progress. You could take away work to mark for the parents and provide copies of sample exam papers you may be using for other children. There are many flexible variations that you could adopt to increase your business during the day without disturbing your regular work in the evenings.

So that parents do not feel removed from the education system there are many societies that exist whose members educate their children at home. Meetings are held, at which ideas and experiences are swapped. Such societies are an invaluable resource for parents and children – and also for you if you can access their members. Some venues, galleries and museums included, offer discounted admission if you are educating your children at home. Consider advertising in their newsletters and on their notice boards.

Media Awareness

As you become increasingly involved in private tuition you will find yourself taking more than a passing interest when education is mentioned in the media. As education in this country is not at its best at the moment rarely a week goes by without something of relevance being discussed in the news. Successive governments enjoy using education as a political football but rarely deliver what they promise. Education ministers, (quite aware, as we all are, that something is seriously wrong) love to implement change for the sake of change, which is seldom effective.

Always keep your eyes and ears open when schools are in the news, or when the focus is on teachers who are unhappy and are suggesting alternative methods of educating. Watch education programmes on television and listen to the news. If something catches your attention video it or make notes for yourself. Listen to the radio when driving; you will often catch lively debates or interviews concerning schools and education. Buy an occasional newspaper, national or local; many interesting articles can be found which you can cut out and keep as reference.

You need to be aware of any changes happening that may affect private home tutoring. Watch the media closely at all times as anything can – and does – happen. Whatever happens to education there will always be a need for private tuition, even if the government radically improve systems and standards – which is very unlikely.

When something important and intriguing is mentioned in the media regarding education, do not be surprised if, when mentioning this to a parent, you discover they don't know what you are talking about. Many parents do not buy newspapers, nor do they watch the news on television. They only occasionally get to know what is happening at school through their child. News may (or may not) reach them through a printed leaflet that the child may (or may not) remember to bring home, or verbally, usually with a distortion of the facts. Therefore, do not always assume that parents are in touch with what is happening at their child's school or with education in general. You must keep them informed.

"Half my GCSE pupils can't spell and can barely write ... but they got A grades."

Use your local newspaper to your advantage. Check who is advertising under tuition or education and ask someone else to ring them up and gather all the details for you, pretending they have a child who needs tutoring. Find out the fee, what they offer, whether children have to be taken to them, etc.

It is always prudent to see if you have any competition in your area and how they operate. You will find that parents frequently advertise for a tutor for their child, so be prepared to ring them and send them your information, a leaflet or a card.

"One in four fails to get even one good GCSE."

The local newspaper will also list (usually as a league table) all the schools local to you who have just received their SATs results. These usually appear in July/August and provide you with important information. If a school has had poor results then target the area around that school by placing your leaflets in shops, post offices and sports centres, etc. In addition, if a school has just received a bad OFSTED report you must try to reach the parents of the children who go to that school by placing your advertisement in shops and venues close to it.

Always be aware of what is happening in local schools. Talk to parents who have attended parents' evenings and, if you have children and visit schools yourself, keep your eyes and ears open when you visit and ask lots of questions. You do not have to disclose that you are a private home tutor.

You do not have to buy lots of different newspapers each day. Many of the papers are online and free to access. If you are going to get a paper the Times Education Supplement is the most focused on education (www.tes.co.uk). Most of the papers are also available for free at your local library. Remember, that any legitimate expenses can be offset against your income to minimise your tax bill so keep receipts even for such small purchases - they really can add up over a year.

Allocate 1 or 2 hours a week for professional development - this could be keeping up with current affairs in education or it could be upskilling yourself to be able to increase your range of subjects.

Keep a filing box and put into it any articles, website details or notes on TV pieces. Have a system to organise it e.g. via stage in school system, date of article or relevance to tutoring.

Exercise:

During the next week watch the news, read newspapers and the internet to find 3 articles relating to national or local education.

Exams, Tests and Grammar or Private School Selection

There is a strong body of contention today, particularly amongst schoolteachers, of the opinion that we must not test or set exams for children. At the risk of sounding like my mother, 'It never did you any harm' comes to mind and I am absolutely convinced we need to conduct tests and exams in order to measure children's progress. Currently too much emphasis is placed on coursework and assignments (which count for 40% of marks) rather than on the exam itself. Yes, exams place pressure on children... but why assume this is a bad thing? Shielding them from pressure is not helping equip them for the 'real' world they enter when they leave school – a world that will require them to find a job. There is a right way and a wrong way to test children in schools and, apart from the shambles of GCSEs and A-levels, I think the government has got it about right with SATs exams. I do feel, however, there may be merit in holding SATs tests at the end of every year from year 4 onwards. If I remember rightly, an education minister did suggest this when he was in office but quickly changed his mind when he found teachers were organising his public execution.

January	Mock GCSEs year 11
Feb to April	Practise SATs year 6
May	SATs
June	GCSEs year 11,
July	End of year exams
Sept - Oct	CAT tests year 7
Sept - Nov	11+ for state schools
Nov - Jan	Entrance exams for private schools

Table showing the annual cycle of exams.
Remember people will need your help months in advance of these.

SATs and CATs

SATs (Standard Attainment Tests) are carried out in year 2 and cover numeracy, reading, writing and spelling. (Just to remind you, a child will be seven years old in year 2.) These tests are marked internally by each school. Year 6 is the next SATs test proper – although many schools give practise SATs for year 4 and year 5 pupils. In year 6 English and mathematics are tested. English tests are in the form of reading comprehension, two written tests and a spelling test. Mathematics is in the form of two written papers, one with a calculator, one without, and a mental mathematics oral test against the clock.

All year 6 tests (children will be eleven years old) are marked externally. The expected average level according to the government is level 4; this completes the child's key stage two phase before joining secondary school.

All SATs exams are taken at every school nationwide on the same day at the same time, and always in May. The results are published in July just before children begin their six week summer holiday.

SATs tests are important not just for the children but also the schools. Results are published in league tables, comparing not only each child's performance individually with other children in the school, but nationally, comparing every school in the U.K. Obviously tuition is very popular from Christmas to May in helping children achieve the highest level. For example, if a child can attain a level 5 in his year 6 SATs tests, he or she is considered above average (level 4 being the norm). Within each level there are three sub-levels A, B and C with A being almost at the next level, B in the middle of the level and C below that. So a parent might say their child is level 4A which would be slightly above average, just below a level 5, if they were in year 6.

Incidentally, approximately 75% of children leave junior school with level 4 ... nothing to get excited about, is it? If a child only manages a level 3 or less then they are deemed below average and 'in trouble'. When children arrive at secondary school their SATs level has a strong bearing on which groups or sets they are allocated. A disastrous SATs result can get the child off to a bad start as they embark on five years of secondary education. It is difficult to climb out of the bottom or low sets if you start off there. Many secondary schools give the children CATs (Cognitive Ability Tests) within a few weeks of them joining in year 7. These are designed to assess the children more accurately, and are taken into account, together with their SATs test from junior school, when streaming them. The tests are similar to verbal and non-verbal reasoning tests (given for grammar school selection) so a failed grammar school child will have an advantage in knowing what to expect and how to tackle the questions.

Most parents are aware of the importance of SATs tests and the streaming of children. If they are not you should bring them up to speed, as this is an annual event and an opportunity not to be missed with regard to either keeping on your existing children or increasing your client base.

In the years between SATs tests many schools still administer their own internal end of year exams anyway, usually in June or July before the long holiday. These are marked and sent home with pupils in the form of an individual subject report.

GCSE Exams

The next most important exams, of course, are GCSEs. Is there anyone out there who still does not believe that standards have dropped? I can assure you quite categorically that they have. And quite dramatically too. It is now possible to attain a GCSE in mathematics having only got 20% of the questions correct. Albeit this is a grade 'F' at foundation level but earlier generations (before GCSEs were introduced) had to get at least 40% in their exams to pass. Not only are the grades, marks, passes and failures completely misleading but it is also the quality of knowledge that is unbelievably poor. Mathematics and English are in the biggest decline. Many of the fifteen year and sixteen year old children I tutor in these two subjects are so lacking in the basics they haven't a chance of getting a good pass grade. The grading system for mathematics is shown in the table.

Higher Level	A*, A, B and C grades
Foundation level	C, D, E, F, G grades
Below this is a U grade meaning unclassified or fail	

Table showing GCSE maths grading system

In English there are also two levels - Foundation and Higher. The school chooses or recommends the level of paper a pupil is allowed to sit but with parent pressure and help from a tutor it is possible to avoid the appalling standard of a foundation pass (especially in mathematics). Most children I have been asked to help were not allowed to take anything higher than a foundation paper. This is where private home tuition is vital to boost them to a standard where they can manage the next level. GCSEs are traditionally still sat in June but many exams seem to now begin in May. A tutor, therefore, has their busiest period between March and May before the SATs and GCSEs. (See guide to school exams and tests.) You will always be busy tutoring children on this annual cycle. Remember, this does not take into account all the special needs children you may acquire or children that just need general long term help without any specific test or exam in sight.

Grammar and private school entrance exams

The last type of exam children need help with is the grammar school selection test or the old 11+ exam. Extra tuition is more or less a necessity in this case, although many grammar school head teachers are not too keen on children being coached to pass the test. From a parent's point of view tuition is essential, mainly because part of the exam involves verbal reasoning, which is not taught in schools, and the child will not be experienced in this type of questioning. The argument for keeping grammar schools has always been hotly debated by successive governments. There are only around a hundred and seventy five of them left in the country and I feel they should be added to, not closed down. If we do not segregate the bright, above average children at eleven years old and encourage them to advance even further, we are in danger of becoming a less intellectual country than we already are.

At any one time throughout the year I usually have five or six children on my books for grammar school tuition. They are not just from the more affluent families, either. However, if the grammar school is a fee paying one, the cost could be between £9,000 and £20,000 annually. If you want to find where your local private schools are use www.isc.oc.uk. It would be a good idea to contact them and find out exam dates and buy some past papers, if you can. I am fortunate to live in Rossendale in Lancashire, close to two of the best performing state grammar schools in the country, both of which are free to attend.

Grammar school entrance exams usually come in three parts taken over a full morning or afternoon at the grammar school in question. Mathematics, English and verbal reasoning papers are given consecutively. Yes, it is hard work and a pressure situation for an eleven year old, but determination and resilience are what grammar schools are looking for in a child. The standard of mathematics and English is usually a little higher than a child would normally have achieved in year 6 (eleven years old), hence the need for a private tutor. The child needs introducing to verbal reasoning and to be shown the many different types that could be encountered. No matter how bright a child is many tests and papers need to be worked through for practise and fluency. All three tests have to be passed and the time allowed is not usually too generous so speed is also essential. You can quickly tell if a child is grammar school material or not and you must be honest with the parents either way. It is unfortunate if a child just scrapes through then struggles in a grammar school for five years. A grammar school environment demands harder work from its pupils than a normal comprehensive school, with a lot more homework involved - equivalent to secondary schools in the 1960s.

As a home tutor you will need to acquaint yourself with verbal reasoning and obtain a couple of books on the subject. Buy different ones so you have a good variety as grammar schools do vary slightly in the style and content of their test papers. Most grammar schools will send out packs including sample papers before the test; these are useful. (If you have trouble obtaining test papers or the verbal reasoning tests we can supply these – see the back of the book.) Most children enjoy the 'new' subject – I usually tell them that verbal reasoning in a cross between maths and English with an assortment of puzzles. In essence this is the case, so children are encouraged to think laterally and logically - attributes grammar schools are looking for in today's eleven year olds.

It is a rewarding feeling to have tutored a child through any test or exam, but I have found it particularly so in helping a child earn a grammar school place. Do this and you will have been instrumental in changing the child's life completely and, of course, in making the parents feel extremely proud. I am currently helping an eleven year-old girl with her 11+ tuition, having been successful in getting her two older brothers through to the same grammar school over a period of five years. Can you think of any other job which, if you do it well, allows you to experience so much pride, satisfaction and appreciation? Neither can I.

Example verbal reasoning questions (from Fifth papers in verbal reasoning published by Bond).

---

1. If the code for BREAKDOWN is abcdefghi, what are the codes for the following words?
(a) DROWN   (b) OWNER   (c) BROKE

2. Find the two missing numbers in the following sequences.
(a) 55 __ __ 43 41 40   (b) __ 8 11 12 15 __

3. Weak is to frail as strong is to (young, old, powerful, rope)

Numeracy

I write this section with controlled anger as I consider the methods some primary schools have adopted in order to teach children basic mathematics – many of which are nothing short of crazy. On reflection I should not be too outraged as these methods are the main reason I am constantly busy! Educationalists, especially mathematicians, are obsessed with change for the sake of change. Schools have taught methods that have worked well for over a hundred years – so if it ain't broke, why fix it?

In the following pages I will review the current arithmetic methods taught in schools. You need to be familiar with these in order to form your own opinion. Time and again I find that children are confused (but not as confused as their parents) by these so-called 'easier' methods. Most children, in my experience, take longer over the new methods and invariably get the answers wrong anyway. Let's begin with simple addition and subtraction, or 'hundreds, tens and unit' sums as they used to be known. You may have to study this new method (example 1a) for a few minutes in order to realise what is happening. Do you feel that this is easier for a child to set out and get right than the traditional method (example 1b)?

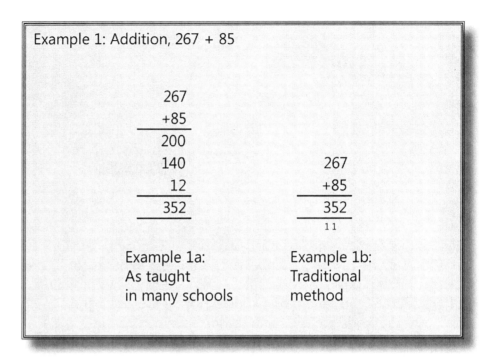

Example 1: Addition, 267 + 85

```
    267
    +85
   ────
    200
    140
     12                  267
   ────                   +85
    352                  ────
                          352
                           11
```

Example 1a: Example 1b:
As taught   Traditional
in many schools   method

Consider the first method: on the first line the 200 portion of 267 has been written. On the second line the 60 and 80 portions of the two initial numbers are added together to make 140 (the child has to complete this in their head). Then, on the third line, the 7 and 5 parts of the initial numbers are added together to make 12. These three lines are finally added up to give the answer... simple, isn't it?

Not only do children take longer over this method, they are more prone to making mistakes because they have more numbers to write down. Do we really believe that a child aged eight and nine years old cannot 'take on board' the complexities of carrying a number to the next column?

Now for subtraction. The new method (example 2a) is called partitioning without exchange. "What?" I hear you ask – those are some nice, short words for a seven year old to understand.

Again, do you feel this is a less complicated method of subtraction than the accepted, traditional method (example 2b)? What could be easier?

Example 2: Subtraction, 563 – 241

$$500 + 60 + 3$$
$$\underline{-200 + 40 + 1}$$
$$\underline{300 + 20 + 2} = 322$$

$$563$$
$$\underline{-241}$$
$$\underline{322}$$

Example 2a:
Partitioning
without exchange

Example 2b:
Traditional
method

Following is another example of a subtraction sum (example 3) performed using partitioning and decompositioning with exchange.

Is it any wonder I am so busy? Have the educationalists any idea how long it takes a seven year old just to set out a sum like these above – not to mention understanding it and getting it right?

You will remember the traditional method whereby you had to 'borrow' one from the column to the left.

Which sum is more compact, less trouble and with fewer figures to write down?

Example 3: Subtraction, 754 − 286

```
    700+50+4                              then      400
   -200+80+6                                         60
    700+40+14   (adjust from tens to units)          +8
   -200 +80+ 6                                       468
    600+140+14  (adjust from hundreds to tens)
   -200+ 80+ 6
    400+ 60 + 8
```

Example 3a: Subtraction using partitioning and decomposition

```
    6  14  1
    7  5  4
   -2  8  6
    4  6  8
```

Example 3b: Same subtraction done via borrowing, the traditional method

Here is another variation on a subtraction sum; marginally less work than the horrific new method shown in the previous example, but still more work than the traditional method. Again, you will have to study the method example 4 for a few moments to realise what is happening. The first line is rounding up 175 to 180 by adding 5. The second line shows rounding up to 200 by adding 20, the third line rounding up to 300 by adding 100 and finally, adding 34 to get up to 334. The four lines are then added up to give the answer as 159... simple, isn't it?

Example 4: Subtraction 334 − 175

```
    334
  − 175
    +5   =180
   +20   =200
  +100   =300
  + 34   =334
    159
```

If you think previous examples were fun wait until you see what has been done to long multiplication. Here are two examples, which have been formulated, presumably, to make things easier for children today. Can you follow this method (example 5)? Neither can children.

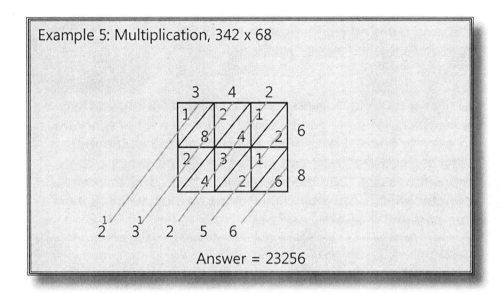

Example 5: Multiplication, 342 x 68

Answer = 23256

Example 6 illustrates a further method. This second of these methods seems slightly easier to understand but a child is expected to add large numbers horizontally and still encounter a carry number in the final addition. Most junior children I know would take ten minutes to draw the grids for the above methods before writing down any numbers.

Example 6: Multiplication, 56 x 27

x	50	6
20	1000	120
7	350	42

$$1000 + 120 = 1120$$
$$350 + 42 = +392$$
$$\text{Answer} \quad 1512$$

To bring some sanity back into the proceedings with the traditional method (example 7) which has served us well for years. The only part of this a child needs to be careful with is the placing of a zero on the second line before starting to multiply. The method and absence of work involved for the child bares no comparison to any of the previous so-called 'easier' methods.

Example 7:
Traditional multiplication
76 x 18

$$
\begin{array}{r}
76 \\
\times\ 18 \\
\hline
608 \\
+\ 760 \\
\hline
1368 \\
\end{array}
$$

Lastly we come to division. Traditional long division, you may remember, was quite cumbersome and took a lot of space up in exercise books. I remember as a child my father committing what seemed like hours and hours to make me practise these monstrous sums. Over the years most schools and children adopted what is correctly named short division, which is more compact and quicker to perform.

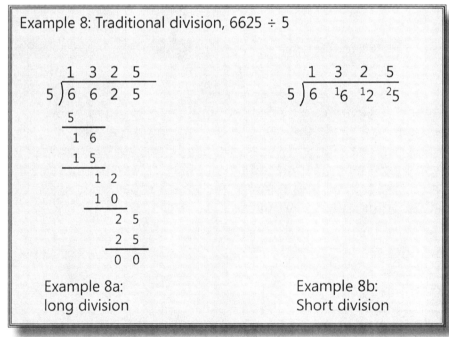

Example 8: Traditional division, 6625 ÷ 5

Example 8a: long division

Example 8b: Short division

Example 9 is a method used at one school in my area. I feel 'no comment' is relevant here, except to say I am currently helping five children who attend this school with their mathematics. One child recently told me the answer to a sum he had just done was one hundred and eighty twelve, rather than 192. I rest my case.

Example 9: Division, 256 ÷ 7
Used in a local school

```
    256
  – 70        (10 x 7)  3 subtractions of
   186                  multiplications by 10
  – 70        (10 x 7)
   116
  – 70        (10 x 7)
    46
  – 42         (6 x 7)  1 subtraction of  6 x 7
     4
```

From the above we have 3 lots of 10 and one lot of 6 =
30 + 6 = 36 so the answer is 36 remainder 4

Exercise: New and old.

To help the students you really should understand how
they are trying to do the sums, so here's a challenge -
have a go at the following without your calculator.
First try the way the kids are do at school now and then
do the sums the way you were taught.

1. 4587 + 2473
2. 3412 - 2738
3. 369 x 78 (use the method in ex 5)
4. 672 x 64 (use the method in ex 6)
5. 7842 ÷ 7

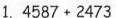

After ploughing through the previous pages of this section on
numeracy you may at this stage feel the need to go and lie
down in a darkened room. Either that or to bang your head
against a wall and pour yourself a large glass of wine. I have a
theory about the increase in arson attacks on schools today. I
don't think children are responsible – I think it could be their
parents.

"Pass mark in maths is just 15%

Proof GCSEs are dumbing down.

Students .... managed to achieve C results by scoring as little as 15 per cent of the overall marks available.*"*

Seriously, though, not only do most children I come across have a problem with these new methods, but their parents also find it difficult to help them. Most parents can eventually understand the methods but they are alien to the way they were taught arithmetic. If you are to become a good tutor you need to be aware of these new methods, just in case you come across them. Not all schools adopt them, however. Some still teach the traditional methods that many parents know and understand. This lack of consistency across the system is not to be desired (presently each local education authority or head of maths decides which methods children should be taught), especially when all children in the UK in year 6 take the same national SATs examination.

I have found over the years that the most common areas in which children always seem to need help are:- fractions, decimals, telling the time, percentages, long multiplication and division (hardly surprising) and tables. In secondary school the older children still encounter these same problems, plus others in the areas of algebra, ratio, area and volume, Pythagoras and most facets of geometry and trigonometry.

A relatively new topic in Maths has appeared since I took my GCEs – probability. This is usually quite basic, involving coins or dice and doesn't pose many problems for children. You will, however, need to acquaint yourself with probability as it may be alien to you – especially if you are over forty years old. There is a significant emphasis these days on teaching data handling and statistics in schools; in fact, some GCSE exams are solely statistical. Hardly surprising, I suppose, in an age of IT.

The calculator has caused such a dependency with fifteen and sixteen year olds currently taking GCSEs that they reach for one halfway through a complex maths problem to find out what 7 x 4 is. Today's generation of children will confidently write down £240 for a calculation they have just done using a calculator – rather than the correct answer of £2.40. Because the numbers in the screen read 240 no bells will ring in their heads to warn them the answer is way out. I am not a fan of the calculator and, in fact, it appears I am not alone, as the instrument is now banned in many junior schools. Children obviously need one in the latter years of secondary school to execute sine, cosine and tangent plus Pi, square root and percentages. Children MUST be taught their tables thoroughly in primary school. Tables are the basis of all future maths they will come across but, unfortunately, not many children know ALL their tables very well.

All schools say they have a policy to teach tables between Year 2 and Year 6 but it is certainly not working. As proof of this try asking any child you come across a few tables questions (even secondary school children) – perhaps your own children or grandchildren.

I sometimes ask young children if they know their 2 x tables and they look at me confidently and say of course they do. They will then very quickly rhyme off 2, 4, 6, 8, 10, 12 and so on. I stop them and say, "very good but those are the answers to the 2 times table. Do you know what 7 times 2 is?" If they do not answer 14 within a few seconds I suggest they don't know them very well, as anyone can count in twos. I have a unique way of teaching tables to children which I have developed using cards.

Nearly every child I visit is given one of the tables grids shown at the end of this section. These are very useful as tables up to 12 are shown in a compact way. I also show the child how to divide using the grid. If you highlight the top line of numbers 1-12 and the first left vertical line of numbers 1-12, this makes it easier for younger children to read off. Please do feel free to copy the one at the end of the chapter.

I cannot stress the importance of tables too highly. Don't assume children know them – they don't. Spend time with them practising with the tables grid and constantly conduct verbal tests, asking them an assortment of tables questions during nearly every visit. Repetition is the only way tables stick in a child's memory – it certainly worked for my generation – but schools haven't time for 'old fashioned' methods any more.

As we move with increasing speed into an IT age a child's basic knowledge of facts (not just in maths) is not simply being neglected – it is, in fact, being eradicated. Dictionaries may

"our kids are sum dunces

Only ONE in a hundred 13 and 14 year olds passed an international maths test, compared to one in four in Poland and one in five in Singapore."

become extinct within ten years. They are rarely used now by school children. Do not assume that children can tell the time. I have come across many bright children who cannot tell the time using a clock or a watch with fingers. I can sense hundreds of you out there nodding your heads in agreement with what I am saying – but nothing much is being done about the problem in schools. If you become a private home tutor after reading this book, you can help change the situation for those individual lucky children whose parents can afford to seek tuition.

As a footnote to this section on maths (or numeracy, as schools now prefer to call it) I'd like to draw your attention to a few actual questions based on a recent GCSE Maths Foundation paper. This should convince you that standards have dropped alarmingly. If you still don't believe me ask employers faced with taking on school leavers with these GCSE passes how efficient their younger staff are at mathematics. Many big companies, such as Sainsbury's, have their own numeracy program to help staff reach basic standards.

GCSE maths questions (foundation level)

Answer all questions

1.

Alex arrives at the bus station at the time shown on the clock above.
(a) Write down the time shown. _____ (1 mark)
The bus arrived 30 minutes later.
(b) Draw hands on the clock face below to show when the bus arrived. (1 mark)

(c) Write this same time as it would be on a 24 hour clock
(i) in the morning. _____
(ii) in the evening. _____
(2 marks)

2.

12	7	58
15	24	31
102	40	92
70	57	43

From the numbers in the shape above, write down
(i) those numbers that 2 will divide into exactly.   _____
(ii) those numbers that 10 will divide into exactly.   _____
(iii) the number that is double one of the other numbers.   _____
                                                            (3 marks)

3.

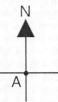

Alison is standing at A. She is facing North.
She turns anticlockwise through 1 right angle.
(a) In what direction is she now facing?   _____ **(1 mark)**

Later Alan stands at A. He is facing South.
He turns clockwise through 1½ right angles.
(b) In what direction is he now facing?   _____ **(1 mark)**

4.

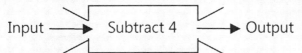

Input ⟶ Subtract 4 ⟶ Output

The diagram shows a "Subtract 4" machine. Complete the table.

Input	Output
7	3
8	_____
_____	16
_____	25

                                                            (3 marks)

Multiplication tables

1	2	3	4	5	6	7	8	9	10	11	12
2	4	6	8	10	12	14	16	18	20	22	24
3	6	9	12	15	18	21	24	27	30	33	36
4	8	12	16	20	24	28	32	36	40	44	48
5	10	15	20	25	30	35	40	45	50	55	60
6	12	18	24	30	36	42	48	54	60	66	72
7	14	21	28	25	42	49	56	63	70	77	84
8	16	24	32	40	48	56	64	72	80	88	96
9	18	27	36	45	54	63	72	81	90	99	108
10	20	30	40	50	60	70	80	90	100	110	120
11	22	33	44	55	66	77	88	99	110	121	132
12	24	36	48	60	72	84	96	108	120	132	144

For students who are confident of their 2, 5, 10 and 11 (up to 99) times tables and by only showing one half of the table this can be simplified to:

1	2	3	4	5	6	7	8	9	10	11	12
2											
3		9	12		18	21	24	27			36
4			16		24	28	32	36			48
5											
6					36	42	48	54			72
7						49	56	63			84
8							64	72			96
9								81			108
10											
11										121	132
12										132	144

Literacy

English (or literacy as primary schools prefer to call it) has changed probably more than Maths in the way it is now taught in schools. In the 50s, 60s and 70s a greater emphasis was placed on what I call the 'mechanics' of the English language, especially in secondary schools – parts of speech, verbs, nouns, adjectives, antonyms, synonyms, metaphors, similes, etc. My experience of secondary schools is that English language is currently woefully neglected in favour of the literature side of English i.e. reading stories and books as a whole class project. This has a necessary place, of course, but not at the expense of every other facet of the subject.

If you think I'm exaggerating ask a typical school leaver to string together a few sentences either verbally or in writing, then check them for punctuation and spellings or just making plain sense.

I think the problems can be tracked back to primary school where Reception and year 1 are taught to read. Most children of my generation could read before they went to school, an aptitude very rarely exhibited today. Children, in my experience, see the first letter of a word and tend to guess the whole word. They do not seem to be able to, nor are they encouraged to, 'attack' the word by breaking the separate sounds and syllables down.

When I am called in specifically to help a child with English, which cases represent only around 20% of my total client base, the reasons vary depending on the age of the child. A year 3 or 4 child (seven or eight years old) could be lagging behind in

"Teenagers' literacy in new slump

The Government's drive to boost literacy among secondary school children faltered this year, national tests showed yesterday."

"Crisis in Literacy

Illiteracy among youngsters is higher that before the First World War, despite the recent burst of effort to improve the nation's reading and writing skills."

reading and spelling – and this usually applies to boys. In year 5 and 6 (ten or eleven years old) the common problems, again usually with boys, are comprehension and story writing skills.

In secondary schools the written and comprehension work of both boys and girls tends to deteriorate right up to the SATs tests in year 9 and on to GCSEs in year 11.

I have a friend who is a French teacher at a secondary school. She constantly complains she has to teach her year 7 pupils English before she dare begin teaching them French.

Private home tuition can improve this situation by again enforcing the basics – practising story writing and comprehension skills and becoming familiar with parts of speech and punctuation. Many children I visit, of all ages, can read and understand a passage reasonably well. The problem is they have great difficulty in answering the questions, because they cannot express themselves properly on paper i.e. putting the answer in their own words when the question demands. Story writing is also a problem – again mostly for boys – due largely to their laziness in not wanting to spend ten minutes doing a simple plan before they begin writing. They also don't feel confident in expressing their ideas (which are sometimes very good) on paper because they cannot spell or punctuate very well.

We are all guilty of poor punctuation, spelling and grammar – none more so than myself, but getting it absolutely perfect doesn't seem as important in today's society of emails, computers and texting. At the risk of sounding 'old-fashioned' again I think computers have played their part in the deterioration of English in today's children. Letter writing skills are disappearing, replaced by quick e-mail notes, and even the art of conversation is being replaced by the nonsense of texting. Have you seen the way children text each other? No wonder their spelling doesn't improve.

Case study:

I had an interesting conversation with an English teacher some years ago whilst at a parents' evening held at a school. My daughter in year 10 complained that when she got up from her desk to walk over to the shelf at the back of the classroom she was often jeered and mocked by other class members – mainly the boys. The purpose of her walk was to go and get a dictionary from the thirty or so stacked together and gathering dust due to lack of use. The teacher's reaction was to explain that she couldn't get the children to use a dictionary these days. They couldn't be bothered or were embarrassed to be seen trying too hard. Before I answered her I took a deep breath and mentally counted to ten, aware of my wife kicking me under the table in an attempt to calm me down. With some degree of sarcasm I informed the teacher that I had a brilliant idea that would help her do her job properly. Before the start of each lesson I suggested she place a dictionary (after blowing the dust off them) on every desk before the pupils came into the classroom. They would then be able to use them, if they so wished, without fear of ridicule and the boys who jeered probably wouldn't notice they were there anyway. She just smiled and nodded but within a fortnight my daughter came home from school one day and said, "Guess what happened today in English, Dad?"

Understanding phonics

Phonics is one of the most fundamental concepts in early teaching of reading and writing. Depending on your age you may have been taught phonics in school but if you went through the primary system before the mid 1970's then it is more likely that you were taught more visually. You see a word and either there is a picture to tell you what it is or an adult helps you identify the word the first time.

Phonics is a simple idea - letters are pronounced the same way they are used in most words. So whereas you may have been taught to say B as bee, in phonics it is pronounced buh. If you're not sure how the letters should sound then search for "phonic sounds mp3" on the web to find a sound file or ask a young person to run through the alphabet with you.

You have your basic 26 letters of the phonic alphabet but there is also the idea of common pairs or triplets of consonants and these are known as **blends** if both letters are sounded (as in fl, cr, pl) and **diagraphs** if the new combination is a single new sound (such as ch, sh, th) and during key stage one and early key stage two most teachers will work through these blends/ diagraphs as if they were separate letters of the alphabet. Most children will only use the word blend.

Many workbooks are available from bookshops or on the internet covering phonics. Following is a brief outline of the most common blends and diagraphs, which you are welcome to copy.

Blend/ diagraph	Example	Can you find 3 more words?
bl	**bl**ack	
br	**br**illiant	
cl	**cl**ear	
cr	**cr**own	
ch	**ch**urch	
dr	**dr**eam	
fl	**fl**y	
fr	**fr**ont	
gl	**gl**ue	
gr	**gr**eat	
nd	sa**nd**	
nt	se**nt**	
pl	**pl**ant	
pr	**pr**oud	
sh	**sh**ed	
sl	**sl**ight	
sm	**sm**all	
sn	**sn**ail	
sp	**sp**ill	
st	**st**op	
th	**th**ink	
tr	**tr**ain	
scr	**scr**atch	
shr	**shr**ed	
spl	**spl**ash	
spr	**spr**ing	
squ	**squ**eal	
str	**str**ong	
thr	**thr**ee	

Grammar

"Simple words 11 year olds just can't spell

More than half the country's 11 year olds cannot spell basic words a shock report revealed yesterday. "Parents and employers will be horrified that 11 year olds haven't learned to spell a fairly regular words like effortless, escaping, realistic, special, planned, qualified and knowledge.""

When you begin your tutoring and you are asked to help a child with English try this simple test. Take out a blank piece of paper and write these four words as headings leaving four or five lines between each:

➢ noun

➢ adverb

➢ adjective

➢ verb

Ask the child to write under each word the definition of that word and a couple of examples. You will get a shock. I have tried this on hundreds of children over the years from eight to sixteen years old, the later children being the worst at getting it right. I can honestly say only a handful ever get this exercise completely correct. I asked one very bright sixteen year old girl, who was due to take her GCSEs in a month, to do this simple exercise. She only answered one out of the four and put that in the wrong place. This is very sad and indicative of the standard of English in our schools today.

Having 'harped on' too much about the English language I have failed to mention literature. Yes, Macbeth, Romeo and Juliet and Twelfth Night are still doing the rounds in schools. I'm not sure whether we should be inflicting Shakespeare on our fifteen and sixteen year olds. It goes against my old fashioned ways, I know – and the words 'heritage' and 'culture' spring to mind. I find, however, that many children I visit find the Bard difficult – especially Asian pupils. Private home tuition certainly has an advantage here in that it is possible to spend time studying and discussing a piece with a child on a one-to-one basis, rather than in the clamour and distraction of a classroom.

Exercise: How's your grammar?

Can you fill in the following table?
If you've struggled to remember these things - don't worry just get a book on English grammar and refresh your skills. You are welcome to copy the sheets to use with your students.

Grammar term	Definition	Examples
noun		
proper noun		
pronoun		
adjective		
verb		
adverb		
conjunction (or connective)		
preposition		

Grammar term	Definition	Examples
noun	naming word,	
	can be physical items	tree, car, paper
	but they can also be abstract concepts	cleverness, courage, justice
proper noun	name of a place or person, they start with capitals	Peter, London
pronoun	general naming word - can be used to replace the noun	he, she, they, it
adjective	describes a noun, usually involves your senses: size, colour, shape, taste, smell	big, red, sweet, round,
verb	doing word or action word, ending can be added such as ed, s and ing	run, jump, cry, say,
adverb	describe how the action is done, they often end in ly	happily, well, carefully, beautifully
conjunction (or connective)	words that joining two parts of a sentence	and, but, however, either, or
preposition	words that tell you where and when things happen	on, under, over, in later, after, before

Case study:

To underline the point about computers having a negative effect on children's knowledge, I recollect a Year 8 girl (twelve years old) I visited one evening. She couldn't wait to show me the project she had done for English on Isaac Newton. She presented me with three sides of A4, beautifully done, obviously on her computer, in colour with neat paragraphs of text and sub headings. There were even photographs and drawings showing him sat under the tree with the apple failing on his head. Everything was spelt correctly and the important dates and events in his life were highlighted. This piece of work when she handed it in was destined for ten out of ten and probably a couple of house points. I praised her on her presentation and she glowed with pride. Then 'old fashioned' me kicked in. I took the work from her and asked her to sit down whilst I questioned her about Isaac Newton. I asked her when and where he was born, his background, what he did, why he sat under the apple tree, etc. She could not answer anything correctly, except she thought he had something to do with gravity. The obvious point I am making here is that the only real work she had done was go through an encyclopedia on her computer, press five or six buttons then print it off. I reminded her that in my day we had to visit the reference library, find a selection of books, copy out the appropriate passages by hand, even trace the drawings or photographs from the book. On our return home we had to compile all this information into a project in our exercise book – and through all this effort we could remember what we had done.

Ideas and Tips

Let's now summarise some of the more important ideas and tips you need to consider in becoming a successful private home tutor.

Within a few weeks of starting out you will begin to formulate ideas of your own and to wonder if they are viable or not. My advice is to try them out. You may devise something I haven't thought of yet. I wish there had been someone I could have turned to for help when I began in this area; or that there had been a book like this one available. I started from scratch and, over the years, discovered by trial and error how to make a success of this sought-after service. I perfected the art of private home tuition, giving it the professional edge it deserves, and am now passing on everything I have learnt in this book so you can join the ever-growing body of successful private home tutors with confidence and know-how.

✓ Owning your own computer and printer is a distinct advantage – or at very least having access to a photocopier. Until you are really busy you can buy photocopies at post offices or garages, which charge 4p or 5p per copy. Look around for the best prices, save up your copying so you can do it in one visit, and always run off a couple of extra copies as spares. A decent second hand copier can be picked up from Ebay or Loot from around £50-£100. Most of you, however, will be able to use your computers to produce a master, then will simply run off the desired number of copies on your printer. Your computer can be utilised in many ways to make your image appear more 'corporate' and professional. You can design your own work sheets to use with children; print your own leaflets and/or business cards; and buy Maths and English packages on line. You may wish to take your own Maths or English packages to a child's house and work from them directly on their computer. I prefer 'chalk and talk' methods personally, using a pad and pencil, but some special needs children may prefer a more visual approach. I know of lower ability children who enjoy pressing buttons and the interaction with a screen – they seem to understand the concepts quicker, especially if they have problems writing. Be careful, however, when encouraging a child to do most of their work on a computer as this can result in a lazy attitude.

✓ Be aware when exams are due in schools then word your newspaper advertisements or leaflets accordingly. People will appreciate your up to date approach and you will gain a reputation as a tutor in touch with his or her clients' needs, rather than someone who simply places a general advertisement that neither inspires nor holds attention. Alter or add to your advertisements just before school holidays to tell parents that you are available to help their children throughout those holidays – most tutors do not work during a school holiday and I find parents are eager for their child's tutor to visit their home regularly (especially during the six week summer break). Offer packages that could then be taken advantage of during the day if children are off school. For example, if you visit every morning during one week, charge for only four days, giving one morning free. If some clients wish to pay one month in advance give them 10% discount. If someone recommends you to a friend's child, and they become a regular client, offer them a free lesson or a £10 voucher for a high street store.

✓ When children are on holiday some parents prefer them to be tutored during the day rather than in their usual evening time slot. This may also suit you as it will give you extra space in the evening to write an assessment or visit a temporary client.

✓ You will have studied the sample advertisements earlier in the book but don't feel you have to use these. If you wish you can design your own, but please take advantage of my ideas and wording. I have spent hundreds of pounds over the years on advertising and obviously have discarded the ones that do not work. Do not be afraid of being too hard hitting – I have on occasion had trouble with a couple of newspaper editors in getting some of my advertisements accepted, but generally you will not have any problems. Look at the 'tame' and 'boring' advertisements in your local paper (you should buy these regularly to see if you have any competitors). Believe me, if you use some of these key words and phrases in your adverts, any opposition will quickly disappear...

➤ Don't panic...
➤ Are you worried about your child's...
➤ Fed up with schools...
➤ Struggling in bottom sets...
➤ Need better grades for college...
➤ Are exams and tests a problem...
➤ Underachievement in class...
➤ Schools cannot and will not...
➤ Guarantee get through to...
➤ Make maths fun...
➤ Old-fashioned methods...
➤ Intensive one-to-one...
➤ Back to basics...
➤ Don't waste the holiday...
➤ Is your child missing out...

✓ When you are actually sitting with a child in a one-to-one situation timing what you do and say is so important. In your initial enthusiasm to get a point over you may be too eager to tell them the correct answer. Hesitate and 'bite your tongue' – resist the temptation, even though a silence seems to last an embarrassingly long time. Even let the child make a mistake, then ask them if they have any ideas where they went wrong. Children these days are loath to check their own work when finished (especially boys). Frankly they are lazy and cannot be bothered. Encourage all your children to self check; do not be too quick to point out their mistakes. A point will stick in their heads more effectively if they are trained to find their own mistakes. This is obviously good exam and test technique anyway and one which is rarely found in today's children of all ages.

✓ Another technique I employ occasionally is that of purposely interrupting a child who is quietly working through a sum or writing a sentence. I ask them, much to their annoyance, about something that may have happened at school, or if they are going out the following day, etc. After holding their attention for two or three minutes I apologise and ask them to carry on. As most children are easily distracted in a classroom atmosphere and cannot get back on task easily this gives them practice in regaining their concentration. Some children find it difficult to work if there is any background noise at all. Obviously classrooms can be very noisy and this can result in the children doing very little work. At the home of one ten-year-old boy I visit I ensure the portable TV is on at low volume in the dining room in which we do our hourly lesson. Obviously I ensure he is not facing the screen, but he is gradually mastering his powers of concentration over the background noise. This is helping him cope in the classroom and the volume of his work is increasing.

Exercise: Think of 3 new ideas of your own that you might consider trying when tutoring a child to engage their attention.

....

....

....

What could go wrong?

Private home tuition is obviously a solo occupation so you very much control your own destiny, being your own boss – a luxury most people never experience. On occasion, however, even the best-made plans or intentions go wrong, but when these challenges arise you will be fine if you don't panic. I have experienced all or most of what may happen and, if you heed the following advice, you will be prepared for most eventualities.

Car breaks down unexpectedly.
If this happens you are obviously going to be late. Telephone the client first to warn them of this whilst you assess if your car can be repaired quickly or not. If the fault with your car is serious and you need the A.A. or R.A.C., then, depending on the estimated time they have given you, you may have to cancel some or all of your remaining clients for that evening. If you prefer, telephone your partner at home and they can inform your clients and apologise to them on your behalf. It may be that you only need to cancel your next appointment and can continue on to the others as normal once your car has been fixed. Whatever happens, do not just fail to turn up or to inform anyone.

The client forgets you are coming.
Yes, surprisingly this does happen, although rarely. The child may have gone out somewhere or be late back, eating into your hour with them. In this case you will have to begin the lesson late but you must finish as normal as though you had begun on time, even if you haven't a client to go to next. More importantly, you

must take the full amount you normally charge – reliability must be seen to work both ways. If there are genuine reasons why the child is not there, then it is up to you as to whether you take the full amount but most parents will insist you do anyway.

Clients cannot pay you.

Again, you have to decide whether or not they are genuine. This will depend on how long you have been visiting and how well you know them. Allow them to pay double the following week or if they offer to post you a cheque let them, if you don't know them very well. Some people depend on their partners returning from work in order to pay you and are genuinely embarrassed if they are not back before you leave. If this situation happens repeatedly be careful; in other words don't allow them to run up a bill. Remember, however, that some families may find it difficult to afford you every week, despite the importance of home tuition. It is my experience that the less wealthy families always have the money budgeted for and ready to give to you at the end of the hour. Sometimes the wealthy families need a gentle, polite reminder to pay you when you're ready to leave. These clients often like to give you a cheque for a month's lessons (which is great for your cash flow).

Whilst we are on the subject of money, you are, of course, liable as a self employed person to pay tax on your earnings if you are above the necessary thresholds. A good accountant will therefore be an asset as you take on more clients and become busier. Most clients pay by cash on each visit, but if you are paid by cheque, decide whether to pay these into your own personal account or to set up a separate business account. You could then claim for petrol, motoring costs, stationery, books and telephone expenses, etc.

The child is ill on your arrival.

Every situation is different and it is very much up to you as to whether you decide to continue with the lesson. Obviously the parents haven't had time to cancel your appointment if the child has only just become ill. Some children are good actors and hypochondriacs, however, so beware. They can make a fantastic recovery just ten minutes into the lesson if you are doing something they really like. Some children are genuine, however, and don't want mum or dad to cancel because they look forward to your visit. If they are not too ill just sit and talk to them about what they have done at school, etc., rather than doing any written work and see how they react to the suggestion of work – play it by ear.

Don't be tempted to tutor more than one child at a time.
I cannot stress the importance of this point too highly. In the early days of my business two or three mothers who were friends and wanted their children to have help with their maths approached me. They couldn't each afford my fee so they suggested I tutor the four children together at one of their homes on a weekly basis for one hour each session. As the children, two boys and two girls, were all friends, attended the same school and were in the same class it seemed like a good idea. It was, in fact, a mistake. When you gather four children together (although I made them behave) there is going to be one born leader, one quiet and shy child, one who doesn't like to get anything wrong, etc., – it was hard work. The parents were satisfied as my fee was split four ways, their children enjoyed the hour and all were left with homework.

I endured it for a month then the frustration set in of not being able to give each child one-to-one intensive tuition, which is the only way to be effective. Don't make the same mistake I did. I even refused to tutor identical twin girls together when the parents found they couldn't afford for each child to have lessons. The rivalry between them was unbelievable – constantly bickering at each other for my attention. I solved the problem by tutoring them on alternate weeks. Don't even be tempted to do half an hour for each child on each visit; it isn't long enough to conduct a viable session. There is a tutor, not too far from where I live, who gives a class on Saturday mornings, seeing five or six children at once. Some parents quickly point out that she is less expensive than me – obviously she is able to be. I quickly remind them that if they send their children to her they are not getting intensive one-to-one private home tuition – she is, in fact, running a 'mini school.' Most children need extra tuition because they are underachieving in a school environment.

If a child suddenly breaks down and cries.

You can usually sense when this is going to happen if you are putting any pressure on a child. Don't misunderstand me, you sometimes have to do this to put your point across. Some children are more sensitive than others and as you get to know each child's personality you will gauge whether or not to back off. The child may have had a bad day at school or a row with a parent just before you arrive. It could be they just feel sulky or in a bad mood – children, especially teenagers, can be unpredictable for no apparent reason. Do not be put off by tears. Yes, it can be embarrassing but give them five minutes to calm down then start again. They nearly always respond more favourably after a calming down period, but tell the parents what happened at the end of the lesson, just in case there is a more serious problem or a worry at school. Some children turn on tears purposely.

I recall an eleven year old boy I used to visit. During one particular lesson he was quieter than normal and hard work to win over. I asked him several times if he understood what I was doing with him and he reluctantly mumbled that he did. Then he suddenly began to cry. I asked why he was upset but he didn't answer so I told him to dry his tears and take five minutes 'time out' and we then continued with the remainder of the lesson without a problem. I had taken the lesson at his grandparents' house and, unbeknown to me, they had heard everything from the room next door. At the end of the hour the boy left the room and went outside to play so I packed up and in came Grandad. He paid me and asked if everything was all right. I said the boy had been a bit tearful and asked if there were any problems at school or if he was just tired. Grandma then came in and said, 'Don't worry, he's just like his damn father – doesn't like being told he is wrong.' With that we laughed about the situation, but the grandparents told me not to apologise as he did this constantly at school for attention and I had done the right thing in not making a fuss when he cried. He never cried again on any of my visits and even stopped doing it at school.

Another of my clients who became upset to the point of tears was a sixteen-year-old girl I was helping with GCSE maths. In this situation it was more understandable as her parents were putting her under tremendous pressure to do well in her forthcoming exams and had called me in against the girl's wishes. She did need help with her maths, but it is easy sometimes to forget how the cumulative pressure of a further seven or eight subjects to revise affects individuals. Her mother had insisted she have a tutor and we got on fairly well but one night she had difficulty in understanding a point and burst into tears. She was fine after a short break and we finished the lesson. Do not blame yourself or feel guilty if this happens – at times you need to be firm with some children – parents will not mind.

Difficult children.

Occasionally you may encounter a difficult child. It doesn't often happen as the motivation is there from the onset if mum and dad are paying for your help. I've seen hundreds of children during the time I have been a Private Home Tutor and I pride myself in being able to get on with all children. There are, however, one or two that I would not have minded losing, given the chance. Don't expect to like every child you come across; some are just plainly objectionable until you win them over – some you may never win over. If you are unlucky enough to meet one of the latter type then, again, this is where private home tuition is at a distinct advantage – you don't have to put up with it. A schoolteacher has to face the same children each and every day in their class, but you can be choosey. If, after a few weeks, you find the child's enthusiasm deteriorates or they repeatedly fail to do the homework you set them, finish the lesson ten minutes early one week and have a word with the parents. Tell them of your concerns and suggest that unless the child shows some enthusiasm and interest they are wasting their money.

If there is still no improvement in the child's attitude after a further two or three weeks suggest to the parents that you give the child a rest for a month or two. This gives you the option of going back if you really want to, or, if and when the parents ring you back, to politely tell them all your places are full. Do not feel guilty about this, you don't have to put up with any negativity from any child; no matter how hard you try you will not win over every child.

In highlighting some of the negative things that may happen as you pursue you new career I do hope I haven't put you off – that is not the intention of this book. I simply feel it is important to warn you of any pitfalls by sharing my experiences with you. All the previous possibilities are the exception rather than the norm – honestly.

Exercise:

What would you do if a child suddenly becomes upset and breaks down in tears?

....

....

....

How would you handle a last minute cancellation?
Would you still charge your fee?

....

....

....

Last bits of advice ......

"Business is Booming

Private tutoring is a £100 million growing business - yet it goes largely unrecognised. Parents are often reluctant to admit using tutors and schools turn a blind eye to something that boosts their results."

A few last words on the whole ethos of private home tuition... you are visiting the child primarily to help them gain better understanding of parts of their schooling that they are struggling with. You should not, in theory, have to show them anything new; it is more a case of tutoring them on and reminding them of what they have forgotten. So be yourself; be natural. Let your personality come through. Try to make the work fun and interesting for the younger children and don't be frightened to go right back to basics with the older ones. Do not try to be a person that you are not; if you have a good sense of humour, use it! All children love a laugh and a joke – they will respond to you better – then it's quickly back to the point to underline why you are there. Whatever you do, do not try to act like a teacher; most children have had enough of teachers during the day.

If the child is having problems at school it is important you make them forget about the school environment for at least one hour! In my experience I have found the role of private home tutor is more than just helping the child with sums and words. Just as important (in some cases more so) is the ability to give a child confidence. You will be responsible for making a shy child more able in school, encouraging children to answer questions in class and giving them the confidence to put up their hand when questions are asked.

Many children I visit are quite sensitive and are reluctant to participate in the classroom for fear of 'getting it wrong' or 'failing'. You will be able to give them all round confidence in themselves by increasing their understanding of the subjects they find difficult at school. It is a rewarding experience to see a quiet, shy child begin to blossom, not just for you but also for the school. At the other extreme it is every bit as rewarding to see a child who has behavioural problems suddenly begin to improve in their work – and then in their behaviour. I feel strongly that you cannot educate a child until discipline is present. Unfortunately in schools today bad behaviour and disruption is much more evident. This is not wholly the fault of teachers but rather because of the ways in which society has changed. Many children have little or no respect for authority and this must be traced back to inferior parenting. I feel sorry for teachers; they cannot choose the children they would like to teach or give them up when they are a problem – but you can.

I have been asked on several occasions to become a mathematics teacher in school. Despite the attractive financial incentives that the government is offering, I politely decline and say; 'Sorry, I value my health!' Last year I was asked to teach nineteen to twenty year olds at a local college. The course was quite prestigious – City + Guilds Part III in engineering - containing science, mathematics and engineering drawing. I looked forward to the challenge, presuming that this age group would be much more mature than school children. There was not much difference really; the standard of mathematics was poor, obviously inherited from school, but they had all gained a mathematics GCSE certificate which enabled them to be on the course.

The behaviour of some class members was identical to that of school children, preferring to play with their mobile phones rather than listen to me. I regularly used to send a couple out of the classroom and back to work. I resigned after six months and couldn't wait to get back to the satisfaction of tutoring individual children. If you are a teacher reading this you will understand exactly what I am saying.

Private home tuition is something you can try without giving up your present job. If you are over fifty years old you will

"Private
tutoring
necessary
to fill state
school gap

It is the only
way to give our
children an
equal chance
of gaining
university
places."

know how difficult it is to get another job anyway. This is an ideal age to become a private home tutor – so what are you waiting for? Even if you are financially stable, in retirement my generation must give something back to society. Schools in the United Kingdom are far too low in the numeracy ability tables and not much better in literacy. This situation will not improve overnight but your help as a tutor can help to change things for the better right now. You will never run out of children who need help. Flexibility is your biggest asset, don't forget this. You are your own boss. You can do whatever you like, within reason. You are not answerable to anyone. If you are used to working for someone else, perhaps in the NHS or police force (I have trained many nurses and police officers) it will be a while before you get used to this type of freedom; but you will, and you will enjoy it.

Do not think, however, you can improve every child you come across. This would be impossible and you must not expect it of yourself. If you tutor someone for a few months who does not show any signs of improvement or benefit from your visits stop and ask yourself what the child would be like if you didn't visit once a week. Some children really struggle at school and their parents are content for them just to stand still and keep their heads above water!

In most cases one hour a week is not enough to turn a child into a genius, they must help themselves too. They, with their parents' help, must change their mind set and attitude. You will then see the 'light go on' and a child will begin to improve, but don't expect results too quickly. Be patient and win the child over by talking to them like a grandparent and a friend at first – then show them how to do their sums and words!

All that has been said in this book is not 'Gospel' or etched in stone but is simply good advice based on my experiences. Take it, leave it or add to it! Your personality and how you deal with the new situations you will experience will determine if you will make a good tutor.

Be certain of one thing – a child will never forget you, long after you have stopped tutoring them. You will be a big influence in a child's life. I still remember quite vividly the private home tutor I used to go to when I was ten years old... over fifty years ago.

If you are challenged about being a qualified teacher then please read section two again – and do not worry about it. Politely ask the parents why you should need to go to a teacher training college to learn about class management, primary and secondary behaviour, how to handle disruptive situations and all the bureaucracy and red tape involved in becoming a classroom teacher? None of this is relevant or necessary in becoming a private home tutor.

Be proud and feel confident; you are important! You are not selling double glazing, perfume or household goods – you are doing something highly professional, worthwhile and significant – and getting well paid for doing so!

Hold your head high and enjoy yourself.

My very best wishes for your exciting new way of life.

Graham Woodward

Equipment list

Equipment	Number
❑ Briefcase (hard type)	1
❑ Large pencil case	1
❑ HB pencils	5
❑ 2B pencil	1
❑ Black/blue pen	3
❑ Red pen	3
❑ Small calculator	1
❑ Pocket stapler	1
❑ Correction fluid	1
❑ Small roll of sellotape	1
❑ Small glue stick	1
❑ Pencil sharpener (metal)	1
❑ Pencil rubbers	3
❑ Coloured highlighters	3
❑ Pack of paper clips	1
❑ Small pack of coloured pencils	1
❑ Pair of compasses	1
❑ Small 45 degree set square	1
❑ Small 60 degree set square	1
❑ 360 or 180 degree protractor	2
❑ 15 cm (6") ruler	1

Equipment	Number
❑ 30 cm (12") ruler	1
❑ Assorted post-it pads	5
❑ Assorted coloured card wallets	10
❑ Assorted coloured card folders	10
❑ Clear plastic folders	10
❑ Coloured plastic display wallets	10
❑ Lined white paper pads	5
❑ Pack of plain paper	1
❑ Pack of 1 mm square graph paper	1
❑ Pack of 1 cm squared paper pad	1
❑ Pack of assorted coloured card	1
❑ Pack of reward stickers	1
❑ Small note pads/books	3
❑ Hard backed A4 record book	1
❑ Small pocket calendar	1
❑ A5 page to a day diary	1
❑ Upright rigid file boxes (one for reach day)	5
❑ Expandable file box	1
❑ Upright card file boxes	10
❑ A4 box file	2
❑ A4 ring binders	3
❑ Card clock with removable hands	1

The full list (excluding brief case or a professional looking bag) should cost around £100.

You can get all of this from a stationery outlet like Rymans or Staples but you can also find most of what you need in the bigger supermarkets.

Further reading

CGP books, www.cgpbooks.co.uk, 0870 750 1242
Very good comprehensive worksheets, books and materials for all ages. Maths, English, Science and History. Used in many primary schools and very reasonably priced.

Letts Revision Guides, www.lettsandlonsdale.com, 01539 565920
Excellent books used in both primary and secondary school for maths, science and languages.

Collins Educational, www.collinseducation.com
Practise in basic skills for English and maths.

Schofield and Sims, www.schofieldandsims.co.uk, 01484 607080
Extremely good workbooks on maths, English and science from early years to the end of key stage two.

The Book People. www.thebookpeople.co.uk, 0845 602 40 40
This is a mail order catalogue for all types of books, but they quite often include educational books – mainly Letts – at a considerable reduction from book shop prices!

Bond, www.nelsonthornes.com/bond, 01242 267287
Assessment and progress papers in mathematics, English and verbal reasoning, A good assortment of tests for grammar school selection for all age seven to eleven years in a series of stages.

ACBlack, www.acblack.com/children/
They have a range of books in their primary catalogue specifically covering each school year called get ready for year 1 etc.

If you have any difficulty in finding any of the previously mentioned recommended books, then please do not hesitate to contact us for samples at:

GPW Tuition Services 6, Churchtown Crescent Bacup Lancashire OL13 9PL UK
email: graham.woodward@O2.co.uk.

Useful forms

The forms on the following pages can be downloaded for free from the publisher's website section (www.uolearn.com) on tutoring. We've made them in word format so that you can change them to suit your needs. Please do feel free to copy the ones in the book if you would prefer.

List of forms:

➢ Student details

➢ Initial assessment visit

➢ Student record

➢ Progress notes for parents

➢ Example headings for accounts

➢ 2 week diary

Student Details

Name of student:

Parents' names:

Contact source:

Address and Directions:

Tel:

Email:

School:

Ages & D.O.B.

Year:

Key stage level:

Reason for calling:

Weaknesses and Problems:

Initial assessment date and time:

Initial assessment

Name of student:

Date and time:

Likes best:	**Dislikes most:**

Present school report comments:

Reasoning:	**Personality and first impressions:**
Spelling:	
Alphabet:	
Maths:	
Tables:	**Weakness from assessment:**
Shapes:	
Fractions:	
GCSE level and assessment:	
Suggested tutoring period:	

Comments:

Student record

Name of student:

Initial assessment date and time:

Lesson time and date	Work done in hour	Homework	Comments

Student Feedback
Name of student:
Date(s):
What your child has been doing recently:
What will be covered in the next session(s):
Current weaknesses:
Achievements and progress:

Financial records:

Please check with your local tax office about the exact records you need to keep and how long you need to retain them.

Invoices should have: The word invoice in big letters, your address and company name, a unique invoice number, the student's name, the parent's address, the date of the work and the amount.

In excel you should have at least four sheets - a summary one giving an overview, an incoming money page, an outgoing expenses page and a millage page. On each page have a cell near the top that is the sum of all the money on that page (in the cell put *=sum(D2:D2000)* if say your amount column was in D and there were less than 2000 entries). On the summary page put = into the cell where you want the amount to be then don't press return move the cursor into the sum cell on the other sheet then press return and the amount will automatically move into the summary page.

Incoming money headings:

Date of work	Student name	Invoice number	Amount	Date paid	Paid by	Notes

Outgoing money headings:

Date of purchase	Supplier name	Description	Amount	Paid by	Notes

Mileage headings:

Date	Location	Mileage	Reason for travel

The 'paid by' is for cash, cheque, paypal, credit card so that if you need to check your records later you can easily find the proof of payment.

Things to keep:

All receipts for anything work related, credit card bills, paypal payments, council tax bills, utilities bills, phone bills, mobile phone expenses, copies of your invoices and all bank statements, even non work related ones as you have to give your total interest earned on all accounts.

Monday Date:	Tuesday	Wednesday	Thursday	Friday	Saturday

Monday Date:	Tuesday	Wednesday	Thursday	Friday	Saturday

Index

A

Acquiring your clientbase 24–32
Advertising 24–32
A level 23
Annual cycle of exams 90
AS level 23

B

Books 56, 132

C

Case studies
    Disruptive behaviour 21
    Mail drops 28
    Tutor income 37, 38
    Travelling 44
    Building confidence 66
    Special needs 74
    Use a dictionary 109
    Computer games 115
CATs (Cognitive ability tests) 90–91
CRB (Criminal records bureau) 18

D

Diploma 23

E

English 107–115
Equipment list 130
Exams 89–94
Exercises
    Skills for tutoring 17
    Your income 39
    First telephone call 43
    First visit discussion 54
    Getting organised 58
    Code of conduct 63
    Unusual questions 68
    Definitions of special needs 77
    Following the news 88
    Maths methods 101
    How's your grammar? 112
    Engaging attention 119
    Preparing for problems 125

F

Fees 35
Financial records 139
First visit and assessment 47–53
Forms for you to copy
    Equipment list 130
    Student details 135
    Initial assessment 136
    Student record 137
    Student feedback 138
    Two week diary 140
Foundation level GCSE 92
Further reading 132

G

GCSEs 23, 25, 81, 92, 102
Grammar 112–114
    Adjective 114
    Adverb 114
    Conjunction (or connective) 114
    Noun 114
    Preposition 114
    Pronoun 114
    Proper noun 114
    Verb 114
Grammar school entrance 93–94

H

Higher level GCSE	92
Home educating	79–85
Homework	70–72

I

Ideas and tips	116–119
IEP (Individual education plan)	21,78
Immediate improvement	64–69
Initial assessment	47–55
Initial response	40–43
Insurance	39
ISA (Independent safeguarding authority)	18

K

Key stages	23, 80

L

Leaflets	27
Limited company	39
Literacy	107–115

M

Mail drops	28
Maths	95–106
Addition	96
Subtraction	97
Multiplication	99
Division	100
Multiplication tables	106
Maths revision days	144
Media awareness	86–88

N

National curriculum	80
Numeracy	95–106

O

OFSTED	30, 87
Overhead costs	37

P

Phonics	110–111
Planning a timetable	44–46
Potential income	35–39
Preparation	55–58
Private school entrance exams	93–94
Professionalism	59–63

Q

Qualifications (for tutors)	13–16

R

Record keeping	38

S

SATs (Standard attainment tests)	23, 26, 90–91, 102
Schools today	19
SEN (Special educational needs)	73, 80
Special needs children	73–78
SSAs (Special support assistants)	73
Statemented children	73–78

T

Tax	38
Timetable for tutorials	44

U

Useful forms	134–138

W

Websites for tutors	33
Web traffic	34
What could go wrong?	120–125
Worksheet packs	143

Z

Zany questions	68

*Worksheet Packs

The following packs of worksheets have been designed by the author, Graham Woodward, and have been used extensively with much success over the years to tutor children of all ages and abilities. They are sent black on white, as loose A4 sheets enabling you to use them as master copies to photocopy many times.

If you have any requirements on a specific subject in mathematics or English that is not covered, i.e. from fractions to Pythagoras or from verbs to onomatopoeias, please write to us at GPW Tuition Services, 6 Church Town Crescent, Bacup, Lancashire, OL13 9PL and we will endeavour to help.

To order these workpacks please visit www.gpwtutoring.co.uk or write to the author at the address above.

Pack 1: An assortment of worksheets used for assessment on your first visit incorporating maths and English tests in varying degrees of difficulty.
Pack 2: Sample of Grammar School Selection Exam papers in maths and English from actual schools.
Pack 3: A variety of verbal reasoning sheets for practice in Grammar School Selection.
Pack 4: An assortment of worksheets for progress and revision in Maths GCSE.
Pack 5: Various worksheets for literacy at key stage 1 levels.
Pack 6: As above for key stage 2 levels.
Pack 7: As above for key stage 3 levels.
Pack 8: Various worksheets for numeracy at key stage 1 levels.
Pack 9: As above for key stage 2 levels.
Pack 10: As above for key stage 3 levels.

*Maths Information and Revision Days

You are personally invited by the author to attend a full day or two-day mathematics session here in Lancashire's beautiful Rossendale Valley. Both sessions are intensive yet informal and usually on a one-to-one basis. They are packed with ideas and tips and held in the kind of atmosphere and environment you will encounter when visiting your clients. If you have any self-confessed weaknesses in mathematics from your school days here is a unique opportunity to sort them out. Full details, including available days, times and map will be sent on receipt of your letter.

Full Day Session

On a one-to-one basis Graham Woodward will take you through all the 'new' methods in mathematics that are now found in some primary schools. He will also go over everything children find difficult in mathematics from ages six to eleven years (up to Year 6). Notes will be made for you to keep and packs 8 and 9 are included in the price.

Sessions last from 9:30 to 3:30. Lunch is included.
Price: from £195.00

Two Day Session

The first day is identical to the full day session, outlined above. On day two Graham Woodward will take you through the secondary school mathematics syllabus up to GCSE Level, again highlighting areas many children find difficult. Graham will also help you brush up on your own mathematics skills. Again, extensive notes will be made for you and in addition packs 4, 8, 9 and 10 will be yours to keep.

The price includes overnight accommodation at a beautiful farmhouse with impressive views, set high in the hills of Lancashire's Rossendale Valley.

Lunch is also provided on day two.
Price: from £395.00

Two Day one-to one session on becoming a tutor

Also available is the one-to-one 2 day training course to train you as a tutor. If you want more help you might like to consider the face to face course that Graham offers. It is an intensive one-to-one training package over two days where everything is supplied for you to start a very lucrative business of your own.

During the training session Graham spends two days with you including one night where you accompany him visiting several of his tutees, in their own homes and meet their parents. You can see first hand how it is done, take notes, pick up tips and discuss things with Graham as you go along.

As part of the course you'll be given a briefcase full of everything you'd be likely to need as a home tutor and an assortment of useful books and work sheets.

One of the most special things about taking part in the two day course is that you have unlimited support from Graham to help you set up your business. Price: from £595.00

To apply for a place on any of these courses please contact Graham at GPW Tuition Services, 6 Churchtown Crescent, Bacup, Lancashire, Ol13 9PL or visit www.gpwtutoring.co.uk

*Please note these are services provided by the author.
The publishers, Universe of Learning Limited, have no liability, responsibility or involvement regarding these events and resources.

About the publishers

Universe of Learning Limited is a small publisher based in the UK with production in England and America. Our authors are all experienced trainers or teachers who have taught their skills for many years. We are actively seeking qualified authors and if you visit the authors section on www.UoLearn.com you can find out how to apply.

All our books are written by teachers, trainers or people well experienced in their roles and our goal is to help people develop their skills with a well structured range of exercises.

If you have any feedback about this book or other topics that you'd like to see us cover please do contact us at support@UoLearn.com.

Keep Learning!

Speed Writing Skills Training Course

Speedwriting for faster note taking and dictation, an alternative to shorthand to help you take notes.

ISBN 978-1-84937-011-0, from www.UoLearn.com

✓ "The principles are very easy to follow, and I am already using it to take notes."
✓ "BakerWrite is the easiest shorthand system I have come across."
✓ "I will use this system all the time."
✓ "Your system is so easy to learn and use."

Speed Reading
Skills Training Course

How to read a book, report or short document on paper or online three times as fast with comprehension for study skills and business

Free downloadable speed reading test and workbook
Easy exercises and software reviews to learn rapid reading

ISBN: 978-1-84937-021-9, Order at www.UoLearn.com

Would you like to learn simple techniques to help you read 3 times as fast?
This book has a series of easy to follow guided exercises that help you change your reading habits to both read faster and to evaluate which parts to read and in what order.

Study Skills Training Course

How to pass your exam, test or coursework easily

Improve your learning skills to pass exams and assessments, take notes, memorize facts and speed read, for studying at school and college
Free downloadable workbook

ISBN: 978-1-84937-020-2, Order at www.UoLearn.com

Study should be about extracting the information you need from the sources available as easily and quickly as possible. This book has a series of easy to follow exercises to help you become a super-learner.

Dr Greenhall's techniques helped her to get a first class honors degree in physics and chemistry, a doctorate in science and an MA in education, easily and with little effort. Guided exercises will help you to learn the secrets of these successes.

Coaching Skills Training Course

Your toolkit to coaching yourself and others, with exercises and scripts.

ISBN: 978-1-84937-019-6, Order at www.UoLearn.com

- ✓ An easy to follow 5 step model
- ✓ Exercises will help you enhance your skills
- ✓ Learn to both self-coach and coach others
- ✓ Work at your own pace to increase your ability
- ✓ Over 25 ready to use ideas
- ✓ How to use NLP in your coaching
- ✓ Goal setting tools to help achieve ambitions

A toolbox of ideas to help you become a great coach.

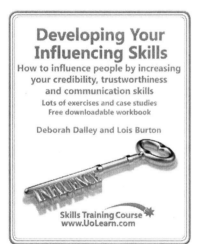

Developing Your Influencing Skills,

How to influence people by increasing your credibility, trustworthiness and communication skills

ISBN: 978-1-84937-022-6, Order at www.UoLearn.com

What are the characteristics that make some people more influential than others?

This book will give you the keys to successfully increase your influence at work and at home.
In this book you will discover how to:

- ✓ Decide what your influencing goals are and state them in a compelling way
- ✓ Find ways to increase your credibility rating
- ✓ Develop stronger and more trusting relationships
- ✓ Inspire others to follow your lead
- ✓ Become a more influential communicator

This book is packed with case studies, exercises and practical tips to help develop the traits required to become more influential.